FRENCH REVOLUTIONS

FOR BEGINNERS®

FRENCH REVOLUTIONS
FOR BEGINNERS®

WRITTEN BY
MICHAEL J. LaMONICA

ILLUSTRATED BY
T. MOTLEY

FOR BEGINNERS®

Published by For Beginners LLC
155 Main Street, Suite 211
Danbury, CT 06810 USA
www.forbeginnersbooks.com

Text: ©2014 Michael J. LaMonica
Illustrations: ©2014 T. Motley

Design and composition by Tim E. Ogline / Ogline Design.

A For Beginners® Documentary Comic Book

Cataloging-in-Publication information is available from the Library of Congress.

ISBN # 978-1-934389-91-1 Trade

Manufactured in the United States of America

For Beginners® and Beginners Documentary Comic Books®
are published by For Beginners LLC.

First Edition

10 9 8 7 6 5 4 3 2 1

CONTENTS

INTRODUCTION

YOU SAY YOU WANT A REVOLUTION?

Allons enfants de la Patrie, le jour de gloire est arrivé! "Arise children of the Fatherland, the day of glory has arrived!" These opening lines to La Marseillaise, France's famously stirring and evocative national anthem, capture perfectly the passion, fear, and frenetic energy of Republicanism's sanguinary birth on French soil. Through the violence of the Revolution, the reign of the Bourbon kings ended and modern France was born. Over the course of the 19th and 20th centuries, the Enlightenment ideals of *liberté, egalité,* and *fraternité* would spread throughout Europe and beyond as ancient monarchies fell, replaced by representative democracies. Of course, the closing lines of the first stanza are: *Qu'un sang impur abreuve nos sillons!* Or roughly translated, "Let an impure blood water our furrows!" Well, just because the ideals were enlightened didn't mean the methods were equally so!

You may be wondering why the title of this book has "French Revolutions" in the plural rather than the singular, and that's a great question. Although the Revolution is often thought of a singular event, France experienced several bloody revolutions and counter-revolutions throughout the course of the 19th century. A constant tug-of-war took place between people wanting either to preserve (or expand on) on the rights and freedoms first articulated in 1789, and those wishing to return to the order and stability of the traditional *ancien régime.* In this book we will examine the constant upheavals and disruptions in France's ever-changing political landscape from 1789-1871.

While most people have some familiarity with names like Louis XVI, Robespierre, and Napoleon, the details of what exactly happened during the French Revolution – apart from pithy royal pronouncements about cake eating and the ever-falling blade of the guillotine – are often difficult to understand, and for good reason. During the specifically "republican" phase of the Revolution (approximately 1789-1799), there were no fewer than seven different changes of government. After his coup d'état on 18 Brumaire (that's November 9, 1799 in non-revolutionary parlance) Napoleon overthrew the Directory and in rapid succession went from First Consul, to Life Consul, to Emperor, to exile, to Emperor again, to exile again, all within the span of 15 years. The next 55 years would see the restoration of the old monarchy under Kings Louis XVIII and Charles X; their overthrow in the Revolution of 1830 and attempt at a liberal constitutional monarchy under Louis-Philippe; his toppling in the Revolution of 1848 and the creation of the Second French Republic; a swift coup by President Louis-Napoleon and the establishment of the Second French Empire; and finally his abdication and the creation of the Third French Republic after putting down the radical proto-Communist Paris Commune (see a pattern here?).

Even more important than the people and forms of government involved were the radical ideas unleashed by the Revolutions. Just think – the divinely appointed monarchy, feudal nobility, and Catholic clergy, which had dominated French public life for the previous thousand years, lost all their authority (or worse) in only three. Enlightenment concepts of popular sovereignty, equality before the law, public property, and inalienable civil rights replaced those of royal, aristocratic, and clerical privilege in Europe's richest and most populous country, permanently upsetting the old order. Few events have had such a profound and lasting impact on Western, and indeed world, civilization, as the French Revolutions. So spread some caviar on a baguette, uncork that bottle of Dom Pérignon, and watch your neck as we explore the French Revolutions!

THE ANCIEN RÉGIME:
WHEN IT WAS GOOD TO BE THE KING

In order to understand the Revolutions we first need to understand the society that gave birth to them. The period prior to 1789, aptly named by revolutionaries as the *'ancien régime'* or old regime, was more than just a political system – it was a way of life that touched on every aspect of existence.

There are two important things to keep in mind while we talk about the structure of the old regime. First, other than political philosophers (who were generally viewed as being either naïve idealists, know-it-all busy bodies, or idle navel-gazers, as philosophers of all generations are), few people at the time could imagine a society structured in a way other than the one they were living in. There were simply no examples of functional representative democracies to draw on apart from classical Athens or republican Rome; and even then, only people with a formal education were even aware of those (which excluded over 90% of the population). Second, most people believed that their social and political systems were not a societal choice, but rather a reflection of divine preferences set down by God. Under this system, everyone had a role to play, and that role was determined by birth. Just as God ruled from His throne in Heaven surrounded by a hierarchy of angels and saints, so too did He ordain the ordering of human affairs on Earth. There was no expectation that the social structure be 'fair' or 'make sense' or 'serve the public good' as we understand those terms today. Society was structured the way it was because God wanted it that way.

So what did the social structure under the old regime look like? In spite of all the changes Western civilization had experienced over the course of the 18th century, France in 1789 still looked remarkably similar to France in the Middle Ages. It was a traditional society that continued to structure itself around the medieval conception of the three Estates of the Realm – those being the clergy, the nobility, and everyone else.

In a society based on divine ordination, it's natural that the prominent role of First Estate would go to Heaven's representatives on Earth: the priests. The Roman Catholic Church had been heavily involved in French life ever since the Frankish king Clovis I converted to Christianity in 496 A.D. From then on, the Church considered the wealthy and powerful nation of France to be her 'eldest daughter' and its kings granted the honorary title of 'Most Christian Majesty.' Much like today, the clergy were responsible for tending to the spiritual needs of the laity and administering the sacraments, but under the old regime the Church had a much larger role to play in society. There was no state apparatus to provide for what we would classify as social services prior to 1789, so the Church took on that role. It was the clergy who were primarily responsible for registering marriages, births and deaths, operating schools and universities, running hospitals, taking in orphans, and generally providing relief for the poor and infirm. The Church also acted as a kind of moral police force. They censored books, sermonized from the pulpit on issues of the day, and of course reserved the right to excommunicate unrepentant members of the flock.

Most local parish priests came from humble origins and lived lives very similar to the peasants they ministered to. The upper clergy – composed of the bishops, archbishops, and cardinals – all hailed from noble lineages and often held powerful positions as administrators and statesmen. Famous examples of this are Cardinals Richelieu and Mazarin, who served as royal advisors to Kings Louis XIII and XIV, respectively. These prelates drew substantial income from their church properties (nearly all of which was tax-exempt) and were extremely influential figures. At the time of the French Revolution, the Roman Catholic Church was the single largest landowner in all of France, controlling 15-20% of the land, including some of the choicest real estate in the Kingdom. For example, many of the lucrative vineyards of Burgundy were owned by Cistercian monasteries (fun fact: it was these monks who first documented how wine is affected by the land the grapes are grown on, a quality known in the wine industry today as *terroir*). Far from being humble men of the cloth, the abbots of the great monasteries controlled vast farmlands worked by thousands upon thousands of peasants, while many bishops exercised absentee control over multiple dioceses they never actually visited or administered. It's not hard to imagine the resentment this caused amongst both the common people and the parish priests.

The Reign of Terroir

The Second Estate, although first in the hatred and scorn heaped upon it by the revolutionaries, comprised the nobility. While often depicted, both then and now, as foppish, powdered wig-wearing dandies who spent all their time engaged in court gossip and petty plots, the nobility based their elevated position on descent from France's medieval knightly aristocracy. Their ancestors formed an elite warrior caste charged with the defense of the realm and who dedicated their lives to martial pursuits. As landowners, they were also responsible for what we consider government functions such as tax collection, administration of justice, enforcement of royal edicts, and maintenance of infrastructure.

However, by 1789, the nobility's military role had been in steady decline for the previous 400 years, as gunpowder, weapons, and large standing armies rendered the expensive heavily armored knight obsolete. Their administrative role had also been largely curtailed with local administration increasingly coming under the control of royally appointed civil servants known as *intendants.* This left many in France wondering what entitled the nobility to maintain their historic privileges, given their reduced role in society.

The Second Estate enforced their preeminent position not only by social custom, but also by force of law. In addition to owning most of the land in France (30-35%), the nobility enjoyed wide ranging tax exemptions and retained a number of feudal privileges. Only nobles could occupy senior administrative positions in the royal court and only nobles could attain the highest ranks in the army. They retained the right to require farmers working on feudal land – even if the farmer actually owned the property – to pay a percentage of the harvest as rent (the *champart*), provide an annual period of free labor (the *corvée*), and to use the noble's mill, oven, or wine-press (the *banalité*).

Much like the clergy, the nobility were divided into upper and lower castes. The upper nobility were known as sword nobles *(noblesse d'épée)* and comprised France's oldest, most prestigious, and most self-important families. Reflecting their traditional chivalric pedigree, members of this order were often the most resistant to change and were the fiercest defenders of hereditary privilege. The lower nobility, known as robe nobles *(noblesse de robe)*, functioned as a legal and administrative elite. Composed of judges, legislators, counselors, advisors, and administrators, members of this class owed their rank to positions they occupied within the government, not to family history, land ownership, or traditional military service. Most robe nobles had been created within the previous two hundred years as French kings sought to increase their own influence (and simultaneously fatten their wallets) by selling these positions to wealthy and enterprising individuals. Not unexpectedly, this created a class division where the sword nobles viewed themselves as belonging to the 'true' nobility, with the robe nobles as nothing more than upstart, *nouveau riche* nobles-in-name-only. Lacking distinguished family names but often better educated than members of the sword nobility, many robe nobles took liberal positions at the start of the Revolution, wanting France to move towards a limited constitutional monarchy with a parliamentary system similar to the English model.

Last in order of preference and privileges but by far the largest of the three orders, constituting over 95% of the population, was the Third Estate. The Third Estate's traditional role was agrarian, made up of serfs, peasant farmers, and shepherds, combined with a small contingent of merchants and skilled artisans who clustered in the large cities. By 1789, the city-dwellers had grown quite prosperous while most of the rural peasantry still lived in poverty. This also created a class division within the Third Estate, mirroring those within both the clergy and the nobility.

The wealthier, urban members of the Third Estate, known as the bourgeoisie, held positions as merchants, bankers, doctors, lawyers, writers, and tradesmen. Educated and ambitious, they formed the upper-middle class of their day. Members of this group controlled an increasingly larger share of the national wealth and were responsible for most of the country's economic dynamism. However, in pre-revolutionary France, money meant little without a title; and unlike the nobility and the clergy who enjoyed expansive exemptions, the bourgeoisie bore a crushing tax burden. While the French Revolution is often portrayed in television and movies as a massive revolt of poor, unwashed peasants rising up against the unjust tyranny of King Louis XVI (Mel Brooks' *History of the World, Part I* springs to mind here), it was actually the bourgeoisie who were the most responsible for the death of the old regime. It's only natural that a growing, wealthy, educated group of people who punched well below their weight in political power would seek to make major changes to the system.

Unlike the prosperous urban bourgeoisie, most members of the Third Estate lived a life of abject poverty in the countryside. To the average French peasant, daily life was more or less the same as it was for his parents... and his parents before that... and his parents before that. The timeless natural rhythms of the passing seasons dictated the pace of life's activities: sowing and ploughing in the spring, tending to crops and livestock in the summer, harvesting in the fall, and finally settling in at home to wait out the long winter (and no doubt make babies). Breaking the peasants' daily toil were various high holy days, saints' feast days, and harvest festivals, all of which provided them with time for relaxation and revelry. While the French peasant was more prosperous than most of his European counterparts, starvation was always just one poor harvest away. Rents and taxes had continuously increased over the second half of the 18th century while wages remained stagnant, leaving them particularly vulnerable.

No description of life under the old regime would be complete without also discussing the figure who sat at the very top of this hierarchy: the monarch, God's secular regent on Earth. The French royal family hailed from the House of Bourbon, who had occupied the throne since the 16th century when the popular King Henry IV ended France's disastrous Wars of Religion by renouncing Protestantism and embracing Catholicism with his famous (and likely embellished) declaration, "Paris is well worth a mass!"

The seventy-two year reign of the "Sun King" Louis XIV brought France to the height of its power and prestige. Faced with putting down an aristocratic rebellion early in his tenure known as the *Fronde,* Louis XIV severely curtailed the power of the old nobility by centralizing authority in an all-powerful absolute monarchy. He famously constructed the massive royal palace of Versailles as a symbol of his authority and nerve center of the Kingdom. Seeking to establish France as the preeminent power both in Europe and abroad, Louis plunged his country into several long and expensive wars. His great-grandson and successor, Louis XV, did nothing to restrain the royal checkbook, putting France in a precarious financial position by the time Louis XVI ascended the throne in 1774.

Bourbon Kings

It is hard to imagine a person more in the wrong place at the wrong time than Louis XVI. A shy, quiet, introverted man more at ease with his model ships than with people, Louis was never meant to be king. The Duke of Burgundy, his older brother and heir to the throne, died at the age of nine from tuberculosis when Louis was only six. At age eleven, his own father predeceased him, making Louis the new *Dauphin.* By age nineteen Louis XVI was King of France. Unlike his grandfather Louis XV – the tall, dashing ladies' man who looked so much like a king you would think he had come from central casting – Louis XVI was short, pudgy, and walked with a waddle. Even a strong leader would have struggled with the enormous challenges facing France at the time, and Louis proved himself time and time again as eminently unsuited to the task of meeting them.

FRANCE IN
THE AMERICAS

The French presence in North America began in the early 16th century with the explorers Giovanni da Verrazzano and Jacques Cartier claiming a huge swath of the continent for the Crown. Permanent colonization did not begin until nearly 50 years later, with the first settlements in Acadia (modern day New Brunswick, Nova Scotia, and Prince Edward Island) and the founding of Québec in 1608. While the geographical extent of New France was truly enormous, spanning the interior of North America to the Mississippi River in the west and the Gulf of Mexico in the south, it was sparsely populated compared to the English colonies on the Atlantic coast. Over the next 150 years, England would slowly chip away at New France in a series of colonial wars before finally delivering the deathblow with the capture of Québec in 1759. Louis XV was given a choice, he could either keep either the more populous New France (about 80,000 people, although miniscule compared to the more than 1,000,000 in the English colonies) or the more profitable Caribbean colonies of Guadeloupe, Martinique, and Saint-Domingue. He opted for the Caribbean colonies, ceding to the English what Voltaire dismissingly referred to as "a few acres of snow" *("quelques arpents de neige")*. The loss still stung however, and was a big motivator in causing France to ally with England's breakaway American colonies sixteen years later (in large part caused by taxes levied on them to pay for the war to conquer New France). Debt incurred from involvement in the American Revolution nearly bankrupted France, eventually leading to her own revolution, and she lost her most profitable colony of Saint-Domingue to a slave revolt in 1791, becoming the Republic of Haiti. Now how's that for imperial irony?

map art courtesy of mapsofpa.com

III

SLOUCHING TOWARD REVOLUTION

What actually caused the outbreak of revolution in 1789? There are unfortunately no easy answers to this question and it remains a hot topic of debate among historians more than 200 years after the fact. There are, however, three broad causes generally agreed upon as catalysts for the Revolution: dissatisfaction with aristocratic privilege by the bourgeoisie, famine in the countryside, and France's looming financial crisis.

The number of bourgeoisie during the reign of Louis XVI had more than doubled since the time of Louis XIV. The nobility thought it was beneath them to engage in trade, so nearly all of the commercial, manufacturing, and financial wealth of France

CUT ALONG THE DOTTED LINE

was concentrated in the hands of the bourgeoisie. By 1789, this amounted to nearly a quarter of the country's gross domestic product (GDP). However, the highest public offices remained off limits to them. Not to be deterred, the rich bourgeoisie did what any enterprising, upwardly mobile social climber would do: they bought their way into the nobility.

The Crown realized it had a potentially rich vein of revenue available to it by selling off minor offices with titles of nobility attached, and the wealthy bourgeois paid handsomely for them. The market value of these offices continued to rise in the second half of the 18th century as demand for them increased. This caused great annoyance amongst the older members of the nobility who took measures to keep these new members out of their exclusive club. The parlements – regional legislative and judicial bodies dominated by the old nobility – resisted admitting these new members and often required applicants to show proof of noble ancestry extending back several generations. In order to maintain the traditional monopoly of the sword nobility on senior military posts, the Ségur Ordinance of 1781 required candidates to officer school to prove noble ancestry on both sides by at least four generations. This shocked both the newly ennobled and aspiring members of the bourgeoisie, seeing the ordinance as a blatant attempt by the old nobility to shut them out of the most prestigious and desirable positions (which it was). Feeling marginalized by a sword nobility intent on maintaining its elite status to the exclusion of all others, robe nobles and rich bourgeoisie increasingly saw their interests aligned. This served to create a powerful political alliance of reform-minded leaders who sought to curtail class-based privileges.

Making matters worse for the good ol' boy aristocracy, the very concept of privilege was itself coming under increasing attack by writers, philosophers, and public intellectuals. Beginning in the late 17th century with Spinoza, Descartes, and Locke, and continuing in the 18th century with Kant, Voltaire, Paine, Rousseau, Diderot, and Montesquieu, the Enlightenment philosophers (known in France as *les philosophes*) sought to subject all human experience to the purifying light of reason. Brought on in part by increasing scientific understanding of the natural world through questioning and experimentation, the *philosophes* brought that same critical eye to the political sphere. One of their primary theories was that social progress is in fact achievable, and that it could be achieved through rational analysis and human effort. While such a statement sounds self-evident today, it was quite a radical concept at the time.

Les Philosophes

Spinoza   Rousseau
Locke   Voltaire   Paine
Kant   Descartes   Diderot   Montesquieu

When the *philosophes* turned their gaze on France, instead of finding an orderly government based on rational principles, they instead saw a bastion of irrationality and chaos. The northern half of the country had a legal system based on Germanic customary law while southern France used Roman law. Numerous overlapping areas of authority existed between local nobles, town councils, regional parlements, provincial assemblies, and royal *intendants*. The Church still pressured the government to censor books containing ideas that ran contrary to Catholic teaching, while law-abiding Protestants had no legal rights in the Kingdom. The King continued to claim absolute governing authority over the entire country without any limit on his power whatsoever. While not hostile to the institution of monarchy itself, they believed that the arbitrary exercise of power based on whim or fancy was both irrational and despotic.

These ideas of natural rights, liberty, equality, and reason obviously held a strong attraction to the excluded members of the robe nobility and bourgeoisie. Coffee houses, reading clubs, and debating societies sprung up in large towns throughout the Kingdom where they discussed these ideas in the open. For this increasingly influential and self-aware class, it was no longer enough for nobles to justify their privileges, or the King his authority, simply by appealing to tradition. All distinctions between people must be on rational principles and serve to advance the common good. The success of Britain's breakaway North American colonies in establishing a republic seemed to prove that progress was possible and that rational people could come together and affect positive social change.

While possessing the least, the peasantry paid a higher percentage of their income in taxes than any other class. Not only did they owe feudal obligations to their lord (whom they might never see), they also owed 10% of their income to the Church as a tithe, a property tax *(taille)*, an income tax *(vingtième)*, a head tax per member of the household *(capitation)*, a salt tax *(gabelle)*, and numerous internal tariffs, customs, duties, and tolls. This heavy tax burden meant that the majority of their income went to food, particularly bread, which absorbed up to half of the average worker's income. When harvests were bad and grain prices rose, that number could climb to three-quarters of their family budget or even higher. This is exactly the situation that occurred 1788-1789.

Throughout the reign of Louis XVI, grain prices fluctuated rapidly. This was partly due to weather and partly due to inconsistent policies. Traditionally, the government heavily subsidized grain and strictly controlled bread prices in order to maintain public order. However, opponents of this policy argued that government regulation of the grain trade was both inefficient and kept prices artificially high. Known as Physiocrats, these proto-libertarians advocated for a *laissez-faire* economic system where a free market in grain would work to drive down prices by encouraging production. The problem was that instead of choosing a consistent policy and sticking with it, the government vacillated between strict price controls and letting prices float on the market. The royal government eased off controls in the 1760s before re-instituting them again in the early 1770s after several poor harvests. In 1775, on the eve of Louis XVI's coronation, finance minister Turgot pressed ahead with his plan to de-regulate the grain trade in spite of the terrible harvest of 1774. Speculation caused the price of bread to spike by over 50% and rioting broke out in Paris, Lyons, Bordeaux, and Toulouse in what became known as the Flour Wars. The government needed to call in the army, arrest hundreds of rioters, and perform several public executions to stop the disorder. Future finance ministers kept the controls in place to avoid a repeat of the Flour Wars until a good harvest in 1787 lead to a loosening of controls. It could not have come at a worse time.

The catastrophic 1783 eruption of the Laki volcano in Iceland killed over a quarter of the island's population and caused a global drop in temperatures. The northern hemisphere was the hardest hit. The resulting famines killed an estimated six million people, making it the deadliest volcanic eruption in history – a record it still holds to this day. France experienced extreme weather throughout the decade of the 1780s with 1788 being a particularly difficult year. The entire country suffered from a severe drought in the spring, and in July, a monster hailstorm swept across northern France, dropping stones large enough to kill people and livestock. The storm destroyed entire fields of crops; it took months to recover from the widespread devastation. Adding to the misery, the winter of 1788-1789 turned out to be one of the longest and coldest on record. Even in the typically sun-soaked Mediterranean regions of Provence and Languedoc, snow and frost stayed on the vines into May, robbing them of their all-important grape and olive harvest.

All of these disasters combined to drive grain prices to their highest levels in decades. As the cost of bread ate up a bigger and bigger chunk of the average family's budget (no pun intended), they had less to spend on other necessities like rent, clothing, heating, and lighting. Many families faced a brutal choice during the harsh winter of 1788-1789: buy bread but risk freezing to death due to lack of wood, or keep warm while they slowly starved. There was certainly nothing to spare on consumer goods, so areas of France that relied on textile manufacturing like Rouen and Lyons experienced a sharp drop in production, resulting in massive layoffs.

Hungry, cold, unemployed, and desperate, the French masses blamed the government for failing to alleviate their misery. After all, it was the King's responsibility to ensure the well-being of his subjects in difficult times. The failure of the royal government to live up to its end of the bargain undermined the average person's faith in the system. As so often happens in times of economic uncertainty, conspiracy theories ran rampant about a secret "famine pact" between the government and a shady cabal of international financiers made up of the usual suspects of Protestants, foreigners, and Jews. When revolution finally came later that year, very few mourned the passing of an old order that had let them down so badly. However, in spite of all this, the regime probably could have survived if not for the looming debt crisis.

While Louis XVI's predecessors had made France the most powerful nation in Europe, an antiquated financial system and extensive tax exemptions held by the nobility and clergy hindered the Crown's ability to pay for its costly foreign wars and extravagant court expenses. Louis XVI's first finance minister, Turgot, warned the King that France's persistent annual budget deficits were unsustainable as early as 1774. Unfortunately, the King blamed Turgot's policies for causing the Flour War in 1775, and dismissed him from service before he could implement reforms. Taking his place at Treasury was the rich and popular Swiss financier Jacques Necker, who opposed Turgot's policies of free trade and financial austerity. In a sense, Necker was history's first financial rock star, becoming a managing partner at a large London bank by age 30. As a self-made businessman, he had a reputation for financial genius and was regarded as the era's Smartest Guy in the Room. A Protestant Swiss in heavily Catholic France, Necker never shied away from playing to the stereotype that he could pull money out of thin air. The fact that his wife operated one of the most influential salons in Paris only added to his celebrity status.

Immediately following Necker's appointment in 1776, there was a strong push among Louis' ministers to intervene in the American Revolutionary War. France had been humiliated in the 1760s after suffering defeat in the Seven Years War at the hands Great Britain, requiring her to cede all of French North America to her historic enemy. The way the hawkish ministers saw it, France could win a potentially strong ally on the other side of the Atlantic, restore her international standing, and most importantly give the British a black eye. Unlike Turgot, who strongly opposed French intervention in the American Revolutionary War, Necker believed that investor confidence in his management abilities would allow him to finance the war solely through new borrowing. He turned out to be right, although the war wound up costing France far more than originally projected and saddled the Treasury with more high interest loans to manage. By the time the American Revolution ended with the Treaty of Paris in 1783, interest payments on the debt alone consumed nearly two-thirds of France's entire annual budget.

As an outsider who possessed the strange ability to capture the public imagination, Necker never had a shortage of enemies at court. As the Treasury continued to float high interest bonds at an astounding rate to finance the American war effort, Necker's rivals began a whispering campaign to discredit him. In an act of financial and political mastery in an act of financial and political mastery, Necker turned the tables on his enemies by publishing the first ever publicly available balance sheet of the State's finances. Diminutively called the *Compte rendu au roi* ("the report to the king"), it was truly revolutionary in that it gave every Frenchman the ability

to scrutinize the Royal purse. Prior to its release, most people believed that State finances were none of their business and trusted its management to the discretion of the King and his ministers. The release of the *Compte rendu* changed people's attitudes; no longer were the finances a solely private concern, but rather a matter of legitimate public interest.

Necker's Balance Sheet

What nobody at the time realized was that Necker had engaged in a bit of creative accounting to make the numbers in his *Compte rendu* look better than they actually were. By only providing the balance sheet for France's 'ordinary accounts,' Necker made it appear as though the Treasury was running a 10 million *livres* surplus every year, when in reality the debt was exploding. He did this by conveniently excluding his war loans, which he relegated to off the book 'extraordinary accounts.' Necker received instant public adulation, both for publishing such a report and for his apparent financial wizardry in somehow running a surplus during an expensive war effort. However, when he attempted to use this popularity as leverage for a promotion into the King's inner circle, Louis refused (mostly due to the Necker's religion and the strong objections of his enemies). Necker promptly resigned in protest.

Calonne, Louis' new finance minister, was shocked when he looked at the books and realized how much the interest payments on Necker's loans were costing the Treasury. Rather than the 10 million *livres* surplus reported in the *Compte rendu,* the war loans in the extraordinary accounts saddled France with a 40 million livres per year deficit that was rising fast. Not wishing to raise taxes any further, Calonne advocated increased public spending as a form of financial stimulus, hoping to spur economic growth and raise tax receipts. While initially successful, deficits continued to rise and Calonne was forced to offer higher and higher interest rates on bonds to persuade nervous investors to buy them – which of course only made the problem worse. Calonne finally became convinced that the only way to reverse France's fiscal death spiral was by reforming the tax code to end the age-old exemptions held by the nobility and clergy.

Turgot had originally proposed reforming the tax code by abolishing noble and ecclesiastical privileges under the reign of Louis XV. However, severe pushback by the noble-dominated parlements led the King to drop this idea. By the mid 1780s though, the long simmering fiscal crisis finally reached a boiling point. The French state was insolvent, needing to take out new loans at higher interest rates to pay off old loans coming due. The peasantry and bourgeoisie were already taxed to the hilt and could not be taxed further without risking mass civil unrest. The only way to get the Treasury's finances in order and avoid a humiliating default was by ending special tax exemptions for France's most well-off. Calonne went about formulating a comprehensive plan to end the crisis.

Conveniently titled the "Plan for the Improvement of the Finances," Calonne's recommendations to Louis XVI were that he cut government spending, eliminate internal customs duties and other barriers to trade, abolish or streamline several indirect taxes, and, the big one, institute a uniform land tax without any exemptions for the clergy and nobility. While interested in Calonne's proposals, the King knew that abolishing traditional privileges would require the approval of the parlements, which was not likely to happen. While a stronger monarch might have just ordered the taxes by decree and dared the nobles to challenge his authority, Louis XVI believed that he had neither the political nor financial clout to impose such an order on an unwilling nobility. Faced with financial ruin if he did nothing, but unable to get the parlements to approve a universal land tax, Louis was stuck between a proverbial *roche* and a *dur lieu.*

Calonne cleverly came up with another way for the King to get this tax approved without needing to go through the parlements and without having to impose it by royal fiat: he would convene an Assembly of Notables to rubber stamp it. Conceived as a blue ribbon panel with its members drawn from a veritable who's who list of the most powerful men in France, their approval would give the King the political cover he needed to implement the tax. This body would have the ability to offer its advice and make recommendations to the King on behalf of the nation. Being handpicked by the King, Calonne expected that they would gladly adopt his royally sanctioned reform plan. Louis XVI agreed to go along with this proposal.

The Assembly of Notables convened in Versailles in February of 1787. Immediately it became clear that this convocation of *grands hommes* with outsized wallets and equally outsized egos would not be the pliant rubber stamp Calonne imagined they would be. Many members disliked Calonne personally and refused to be told what to do by some self-important robe noble. When Calonne revealed his numbers to the Assembly, they were shocked. How could these numbers be so different from what Necker had presented in his *Compte rendu?* Some blamed Calonne for financial mismanagement and saw the new tax as a way for him to cover up his own mistakes. A clamor went up in the Assembly calling for a full independent audit of the Treasury so that they could determine what the real numbers were. After all, with such different versions presented by Necker and Calonne, how were they supposed to know whom to believe? Louis XVI refused the audit flat out as an infringement on the royal prerogative, and the Assembly in turn refused to consider any new taxes until they could examine the books. The parties had reached an impasse.

Calonne

Faced with staunch opposition from the royal court and seeing no other alternative, the Assembly declared that it could not authorize the new taxes proposed. The Marquis de Lafayette, a popular hero of the American Revolutionary War and one of the notables in attendance, argued that only the assembled representatives of the entire nation could ratify such a proposal. In dramatic fashion, he called on the King to convene the age old Estates-General in order to remedy the many problems plaguing the country. The Assembly of Notables had failed miserably and Calonne resigned in disgrace.

IV

THE DAM BREAKS:

THE ESTATES-GENERAL OF 1789

Even before the Assembly of Notables convened, voices demanding that the King summon the Estates-General to address the enormous problems facing the nation continued to grow louder and louder. But what was the Estates-General and why was it in such hot demand? Unlike England, which had a permanent Parliament to act as a legislative and representative body, the Kingdom of France had no such institution. The closest thing it had to a Parliament was the ancient Estates-General, an advisory body comprised of representatives of the three estates of the realm. The problem was that by the late 1780s nobody knew exactly what this body did or how it was supposed to function. Completely

TALLY HO

understandable considering that the last time the Estates-General convened was way back under the reign of King Louis XIII in 1614! Since then the Bourbon kings had reigned as absolute monarchs; deferring to the advice of a representative body (no matter how poorly representative it was) ran contrary to that authority.

Perhaps because the Estates-General had last met so long ago it developed into a romantic symbol of lost liberty, crushed under the lace-frilled fist of royal tyrrany. Like any good symbol, it had the ability to change form from person to person, allowing all to project their own hopes and dreams upon it. The nobility and clergy saw it as a way to decentralize power away from the King and back towards themselves. The Third Estate (particularly the educated members of the bourgeoisie) wanted to use it to end noble and ecclesiastical privilege and make civil positions available to all based on merit. Only Louis XVI and his ministers were opposed to calling the Estates-General since they had the most to lose.

As much as the King tried to avoid summoning the Estates-General, the financial crisis continued to worsen after the debacle of the Assembly of Notables. Brienne, the new finance minister after Calonne, struggled for the next year to keep the government afloat. The great hailstorm of 1788, led to a poor harvest and blew a hole in the budget. When the Treasury attempted to make up the difference by auctioning off more government bonds, even at insanely high interest rates, no buyers showed up. On August 16, 1788, the long awaited and long feared moment finally arrived. With no money left to pay the bills, the Treasury suspended future payments and forced its creditors to accept interest-bearing IOUs. A sovereign default seemed imminent and the markets panicked. Stock prices plummeted, causing a bank run as depositors raced to close out their accounts, fearing the worst. Having exhausted every other option, Louis XVI did the only thing he could do to reassure the markets that change was imminent: he reappointed Necker as finance minister and agreed to convene the Estates-General in 1789.

After the jubilation passed, there was immediate disagreement over how the body would function. When it last met in 1614, the Estates-General was divided into three separate chambers, each representing one order, each order made up of an equal number of delegates, and each order having a single vote. This of course meant that the nobility and clergy, representing less than 5% of the population, would elect two-thirds of the delegates and could always outvote the Third Estate. In the intervening century and a half, regional assemblies throughout France had jettisoned the antiquated idea of voting by order in favor of voting by head, and granted double the number of representatives to the Third Estate. The parlements, seeing the Estates-General as an opportunity to increase their own power and influence, argued strongly against this and demanded that the Estates-General of 1789 be organized the same as it was in 1614. This outraged members of the Third Estate who saw it as an attempt by the privileged orders to rig the system in their favor once again. Even some liberal nobles and clergymen such as Lafayette, Noailles, Condorcet, Talleyrand, and Mirabeau, supported the Third Estate's position and published pamphlets arguing in their favor.

The most famous was written by a Roman Catholic priest, the Abbé Sieyès, entitled *What Is the Third Estate?* Beginning with the iconic line: "What is the Third Estate? Everything. What has it been until now? Nothing. What does it want to be? Something." Sieyès slammed the First and Second Estates as bloodsucking social parasites latched onto the backside of the body politic. It was the long-oppressed and politically irrelevant Third Estate that formed the foundation of the nation's security and wealth. Inherited privilege had no future in the New France Sieyès saw emerging. Most controversially, Sieyès advocated that the Third Estate should accept no less in the coming Estates-General than double representation and voting by head. If the First and Second Estates refused, then the Third should simply conduct their business without them as the sole legitimate representatives of the French nation.

While *What Is the Third Estate?* became an overnight sensation in the salons and coffee houses of the big cities, the privileged orders were having none of it. Facing pressure from all directions, Louis XVI attempted to form a compromise that he thought would appease all three orders, but only ended up causing more agitation and confusion. The King commanded that the Third Estate would receive double representation so that their total number of delegates equaled those of both the First and Second Estates, but he dodged the question of voting by head, leaving that up to the Estates-General to decide.

For the first time in several generations, the people of France participated in a national election. The country was divided into various constituencies, with each electing two clerical, two noble, and four Third Estate deputies. The orders all drafted up their lists of official grievances known as *cahiers de doléances* to guide their representatives at the Estates-General. All taxpaying males over the age of twenty-five were allowed to vote and voice their opinion on what should be included in their *cahier*. It was as if somebody popped the cork on a political champagne bottle; all the pent up frustrations and anxieties of life under the old regime burst forth, and it wasn't just the Third Estate that was affected.

Of the approximately 300 First Estate deputies elected, nearly 75% of them came from the ranks of parish priests. This was a stinging rebuke to the upper clergy and clearly demonstrated that the priestly boots on the ground had no confidence in their episcopal leadership. The clerical *cahiers* reflected the grievances of the common priests and called for positions within the Church hierarchy to be made available to all.

The Second Estate's elections also produced surprising results. The great sword nobles who occupied the most powerful positions at Versailles expected almost automatic election by their peers, and were shocked when they didn't get it. Like the senator who spends all his time in Washington, D.C., only to return to his native district during election season, these nobles were viewed back home as creatures of the royal court who couldn't be trusted. Similarly, the educated, erudite robe nobles were equally unloved and had a poor electoral showing as well. All told, the great sword nobles and professional robe nobles only won about a third of all the seats combined. So who composed the other two-thirds of the Second Estate deputies? They were primarily provincial nobles without much wealth or influence but with strong local ties that ran centuries deep. Given the diversity in their membership, the noble *cahiers* were a confused garble of conflicting ideas. At a time when their order was under the greatest attack, the Second Estate came to the Estates-General confused, divided, and rife with internal rivalries.

Of all three orders, the Third Estate presented the most united front and came fully girded for battle. Although representing all Frenchmen who weren't priests or nobles, the time and money requirements to run for office effectively excluded all peasants, laborers, and artisans. Most of those elected were lawyers, the rest being government bureaucrats, property owners, and merchants. Not surprisingly, their *cahiers* were the most radical of the three orders and strongly advocated for voting by head at the Estates-General, the abolition of feudal privileges, rationalization of the laws, and recognition of the rights to life, liberty, and property.

After several delays, the Estates-General finally convened on May 5, 1789, at the Palace of Versailles. In an opening parade full of pomp and spectacle, the three orders ceremonially processed to their meeting place wearing their traditional regalia – the clergy in their priestly vestments, the nobles armed with swords in their court finery, and the Third Estate in plain black robes. Even their seating was based on order of precedence as the delegates were arranged in a U shape, the First and Second Estates on the sides closest to the lectern and the Third Estate relegated to the back. What none of the sprawling crowds of spectators realized as they cheered on the delegates filing into the palace was that they were witnessing an event that would never occur again. In a very real way, it was the funeral procession of the old order. The *ancien régime* with its hundreds of years of privilege, titles, and traditions would not survive this Estates-General. In a matter of months, long smoldering tensions would finally ignite into full-blown revolution.

After the opening three-hour convocation speech by Necker – which by all accounts was mind-numbingly dull – the deputies' first order of business was to verify the credentials of their members. In a world before driver's licenses and social security cards, this was the only way they could confirm the identity of their membership. What was supposed to be a simple formality quickly escalated into a major crisis. By tradition, the three orders would now separate and independently verify their membership. However, some prominent members of the Third Estate delegation, namely Honoré Gabriel Riqueti, comte de Mirabeau and Emmanuel Joseph Sieyès (the former a nobleman and the latter a priest, but both champions of the bourgeoisie), demanded that the three orders verify their membership in common. The Third Estate was already agitated that the King did not order voting by head and they were ready for a fight. The way they viewed it, if they allowed the three orders to verify separately, they would be implicitly conceding to voting by order. While they couldn't keep the  nobility and clergy from meeting separately and verifying their own member-ship – which they both did on May 27 – they adamantly refused to conduct any business until verification occurred in common. This essentially brought the Estates-General to a grinding halt before it even got started.

Over the next month, representatives of the three estates engaged in diplomacy by courier, passing notes to each other and attempting to reach a resolution to the gridlock. On June 4, the King's oldest son and heir to the throne died at the age of seven. At a time when the nation needed him most, Louis XVI was absent, wracked with grief and depression. While he half-heartedly urged the members to work out their differences and attend to the pressing issues at stake, the tension in the Estates-General continued to mount.

While the clergy waivered, the nobility stood firm against the Third Estate's power play. For their part, the Third Estate had become tired of waiting and, at the urging of Sieyès, decided to push ahead in resolving the nation's business on their own. On June 10, they extended an offer to the other two orders to join them in common verification. Receiving no response two days later, they voted overwhelmingly to proceed on their own. Over the next several days, a trickle of liberal members of the First and Second Estates joined the Third to much jubilation. Finally, on June 17, they voted to officially change their name to the National Assembly and declare themselves the sole legitimate representatives of the French nation. With this act, the delegates had crossed a political Rubicon and were now operating clearly outside the confines of the law.

The King's ministers were shocked when news of this declaration reached them. Some, such as the King's brother, the Count of Artois, considered this an act of open rebellion and urged Louis to call in the troops and dissolve the Assembly. Others, such as Necker, understood the popularity of this new National Assembly and feared that an overly aggressive response by the King would lead to riots in Paris and beyond. Necker urged the King to formally address the Estates-General and urge reconciliation. Louis XVI decided to go with Necker's approach, but to prevent further chaos he ordered the *Salle des États,* the hall where the Estates-General had been sitting, closed until he could address the assembled delegates.

When the members of the new National Assembly arrived on the morning of June 20, they found their way blocked by armed guards and locked doors. The delegates feared the worst; clearly, the King intended to forcibly disburse the Assembly and arrest its members. Having nowhere else to go, they convened in an indoor tennis court on the palace grounds, formally calling the National Assembly into session. Hundreds of spectators – who now had become the norm at Versailles after the Third Estate opened up their deliberations to the public – poured in, anxious to get a look. There, the gathered representatives of the nation swore the famous Tennis Court Oath, a solemn declaration never to separate until they had given France a constitution. In the days that followed, a majority of the clergy and a sizable minority of the nobility (including the King's cousin, the Duke of Orléans) would join the new National Assembly.

The Tennis Court Oath

By the time the King addressed the representatives on June 23, it was already too late. As the Third Estate delegates looked on in stony silence,

Louis XVI annulled the formation of the National Assembly and declared all their acts null and void. At the conclusion of his speech, the King ordered the deputies to disperse and asked them to return the next morning ready to resume normal order. Dutifully, the remaining members of the First and Second Estates cleared the hall, but the members of the Third Estate would not budge. When the sergeant-at-arms loudly repeated the King's order, Mirabeau defiantly shouted that they would not disperse and nothing short of bayonets would force them to do so. A great shout of approval went up through the hall as they loudly reaffirmed the Tennis Court Oath. When the Sergeant-at-Arms informed the King that the so-called National Assembly refused to clear the hall, a grief-stricken Louis wearily waived his hand and told him that they could stay.

This was a decisive moment in the nascent Revolution. By remaining in the hall in defiance of a royal order, the Third Estate had essentially challenged the King of France to a game of chicken – and won. As more delegates from the First and Second Estates joined the National Assembly over the next several days, the King could no longer maintain neutral. On June 27, Louis XVI finally recognized the legitimacy of the National Assembly and requested that the remaining members of the First and Second Estates join them. The Estates-General ceased to exist and the National Assembly, a new body claiming to speak on behalf of all the French people, had taken its place.

V

HAPPY BASTILLE DAY!

n July 9, 1789, the National Assembly renamed itself the National Constituent Assembly and set itself to the task of creating a constitution for France. For simplicity's sake we'll just stick with the name National Assembly since it was still the same body.

By now, news of the newly recognized National Assembly had spread throughout Paris and was beginning to reach the provinces. Nobody knew exactly what the Assembly would do and speculation ran rampant. In a pre-electronic age, most people received information by word of mouth with all its predictable inaccuracies. Imagine a massive game of telephone involving complex political, legal, and economic issues, transmitted over hundreds of miles, extending out over several months, and often spoken in mutually unintelligible dialects by people who knew little to nothing about those issues, and you can begin to imagine the rampant confusion.

The King and Queen realized events were spiraling out of their control and feared that their lives might be in danger. The loyalty of the local French Guards – Paris' resident police force – was highly suspect, so Louis brought in 20,000 German mercenaries whose loyalty he could ensure through wine, women, and coin. The National Assembly balked, seeing this as a blatant attempt at intimidation. The people of Paris also resented the presence of so many loud, beer-swilling German soldiers in their city. Making matters worse, on July 11, the King sacked Jacques Necker – again. Louis's opinion of Necker had fallen to an all-time low after the failure of the Estates-General and conservative elements in the Court convinced him that the Swiss banker's loyalty could no longer be trusted. Once news of Necker's dismissal hit the streets of Paris, civil unrest was immediate. Stirred to action by lawyers-turned-rabble-rousers Camille Desmoulins and Georges Danton, the Parisian mob rushed to arm itself, believing that the concentration of troops and Necker's dismissal signaled a conservative crackdown.

Desmoulins Rallies the crowd

WHAT SAY, FELLOWS? LET'S MAKE THE WORLD A BETTER PLACE! *

HUZZAH!

* I'M SURE IT SOUNDED SOMETHING LIKE THAT.

The rioters vented all their frustrations on the parts of the old regime they hated the most: they tarred and feathered tax collectors, burned down tollhouses, and raided monasteries for food and treasure. As often happens in riots, disorder breeds more disorder. Nobody attempted to stop the rioters, whose numbers soon grew into the tens of thousands. As the King feared, entire units of French Guards deserted their posts and joined in with the rioters. On July 14, after two full days of lawlessness in the Capital, the mob attacked the Hôtel des Invalides (the future resting place of Napoleon coincidentally) and carried away several cannon. Their goal was to use them to take down the imposing royal fortress of the Bastille.

Originally constructed in the 14th century to defend the eastern outskirts of Paris from attacks by the English during the Hundred Years War, the fortress was completely enveloped by the expanded city by the 17th century. Converted into a royal prison by Louis XIV, even this function had largely ceased by the reign of Louis XVI; the number falling to as low as eight inmates by the 1780s (one famous resident happened to be the infamous libertine the Marquis de Sade). Primarily acting to divide the posh Le Marais district from the working class Faubourg Saint-Antoine, the Bastille became so pedestrian it even had its own mailing address: 232 rue Saint-Antoine. However, its imposing appearance and persistent rumors of the gruesome tortures inflicted on the helpless prisoners within made it a popular symbol of royal despotism.

On the morning of July 14, the mob arrived at the fortress, demanding its immediate surrender. The Marquis de Launay, royal governor of the Bastille, knew that he was severely outnumbered and lacked the food and water for a prolonged siege. In the hope of reaching some form of agreement, he invited representatives of the Paris Commune, the newly created 'People's Government' of Paris, into his chambers to negotiate. As the talks dragged on, the crowds outside became increasingly agitated and pushed their way into the outer courtyard, demanding to be let in. While the gates remained barred, an enterprising member of the mob was able to cut the chain to the drawbridge,

opening the way to the inner courtyard. The crowd immediately rushed in. It's unclear who gave the order, but upon seeing hundreds of rioters flooding through the gates, the garrison unleashed a volley of musket and cannon fire on them, killing nearly a hundred. Violence broke out as the mob returned fire with their own guns and cannon taken from the Invalides. Even more ominously (for both the Bastille and the ruling regime it represented), a regiment of royal troops stationed nearby at the Champ de Mars could have intervened and saved the fortress, but instead sat by and did nothing.

De Launay knew the Bastille was lost and waved the white flag of surrender hoping to prevent further bloodshed. It did not save his life. After being taken prisoner, beaten, and paraded through the streets of Paris, he lashed out the only way he could: by kicking one of his tormenters in the groin (go figure). For this unforgivable offense, the mob punished De Launay by stabbing him repeatedly before sawing off his finely-coiffed head and placing it on a pike. They then proceeded to parade it around the Bastille in a macabre carnival-like atmosphere while they went to work on the walls with picks, literally demolishing the ancient fortress brick by brick.

By the next day, news of the attack reached both the representatives of the National Assembly and the Royal Court. This was no mere act of civil disobedience, but outright rebellion. A fortress lay sacked in the heart of Paris while one of the King's own officers was brutally murdered. Louis would have been well within his rights to put a bloody end to both the Paris Commune and the National Assembly – exactly what his hard-line advisors had been advocating from the start. On that very same day, the King arrived in person in front of the National Assembly to a hushed audience. Looking out on the assembled representatives of the nation, the King announced that he had heard the cries of his people and would respond in kind. He ordered the foreign mercenaries to disperse immediately and scheduled a visit to the Hôtel de Ville (Paris's City Hall) to meet with the representatives of the new Paris Commune. From shocked silence, the deputies erupted in loud cheers of *"Vive le Roi!"* and praised Louis as the savior of the nation. On July 17, he met with Jean-Sylvain Bailly, the new mayor under the Paris Commune, and Lafayette, the commander of the newly formed National Guard, where he received the tricolor cockade – a symbol of the New France. Much like in the National Assembly, the crowd erupted in cheering and praise for their liberator-king.

This event marked both the high point of Louis XVI's popularity and the realization of his irrelevancy. For once, the King had acted decisively and contrary to the wishes of his conservative brothers – the Counts of Artois and Provence – who by this point fled the country, joining the first wave of émigrés. Had Louis been made of stronger stuff he could have grabbed the reigns of this early revolution and guided the National Assembly in drafting a constitution that left him with considerable powers.

Les Émigrés

IF I WERE KING, I'D HANDLE THIS DIFFERENTLY.

TO SAY THE LEAST.

TIPPY TIPPY TIPPY

Instead, he vacillated. Not content to reign as a constitutional monarch yet not wanting to come off as opposed to the National Assembly, he adopted an ineffectual policy where he would publicly support the new order while working behind the scenes to undermine it – leading everyone to question his true motives. While faced with few good options, the times required the King to take a strong stand. By failing to either assume a leadership role in creating the New France or suppressing it early on, the King became a mere spectator to the events going on around him. The people now knew that they could openly defy the King and he would back down. Even the outward appearance of royal absolutism was gone; real power now belonged in the hands of the National Assembly and the mobs in the street. The fall of the Bastille announced that the Revolution now truly had begun.

VI

WORKING TOWARDS A CONSTITUTION

When news of the Bastille's fall spread to the provinces, it set the rest of the country on fire. The rural peasantry, starving from the grain famine and paranoid from the conflicting news coming out of Paris, took up arms. Enabled by the success of the Bastille's attackers, many of them roamed the countryside sacking towns, raiding monasteries, and burning noble chateaux. In response, townsmen began to arm themselves to protect their property from these roving bands of brigands. Known as the 'Great Fear,' this rural violence lasted well into 1790, leaving

NO NOBLE CAN ESCAPE

THE GREAT FEAR

COMING SOON TO A DUCHY NEAR YOU

entire parts of the country beyond the reach of the law. Peasants stopped paying taxes and refused to recognize the legitimacy of any feudal obligations. Threatened nobles began to flee the country en masse, causing the first wave of emigration across the border.

This lawlessness deeply offended the sensibilities of the National Assembly delegates. Remember, their membership was largely wealthy and they considered private property sacrosanct. How could they establish their own legitimacy if the country was in chaos? They didn't yet have the support of the military to put the violence down by force, so they needed some other method to pacify the countryside. Already there had been much discussion about jettisoning a variety of antiquated and obscure feudal obligations nearly everyone hated, but perhaps by going a step further they could convince the marauding peasants to return to their homes? During an all-night session beginning on August 4, one of the most remarkable events of the French Revolution took place – the passage of the August Decrees.

The Viscount de Noailles, a member of one of France's most prestigious noble families and a well-known liberal, took the rostrum and moved that the Assembly abolish the feudal system in its entirety. The Duke d'Aiguillon, another prominent liberal noble, immediately rose and seconded the motion. This set off what Mirabeau described as an "orgy" (which he was no stranger to) of legislative activity. Within a matter of hours, the *ancien régime,* with its nearly thousand years of accumulated practice and custom, was gone. One by one, feudal dues, involuntary servitude, aristocratic hunting rights, church tithes, manorial courts, tax exemptions, hereditary privileges, the selling of public offices, and preferential pensions were all abolished or severely curtailed. While the accounts of the delegates conflict on some details, the members all describe a kind of patriotic hysteria as nobles, clerics, magistrates and wealthy merchants rose in front of a raucous crowd to forfeit their various privileges and special exemptions, each trying his best to outdo the last. The frantic session finally ended on a self-congratulatory note in the early morning hours with the delegates ordering a medal struck to commemorate this historic day and proclaiming Louis XVI as the "Restorer of French Liberty."

While it would take several months to implement, the August Decrees accomplished its purpose of ending the large-scale unrest in the countryside. This was the Revolution's first great societal change. While forcing the King to recognize the legitimacy of the National Assembly was a political triumph and the fall of the Bastille showed the power of street populism, up until the August Decrees no real changes had occurred in French society. Finally, all of the lofty rhetoric of liberty and equality moved from the realm of coffee house chatter to actual policy. The Revolution was picking up steam and the National Assembly grew in confidence. For the educated elite who composed its membership, all of their dreams were just within reach. They saw France finally shedding its medieval skin and entering the 19th century as a modern, prosperous nation governed by enlightened rational principles, all under their own steady leadership, of course. With some semblance of peace and calm restored, the delegates could finally get down to the business of drafting a constitution.

The architects of the new constitution imagined a system that would combine the best European traditions of the British parliamentary monarchy with the optimism and enumerated rights of the infant United States. Using the Declaration of Independence as a model, the delegates agreed that they should create a broad set of principles to summarize the basis of their new government. On August 26, the Assembly published what would become one of the most famous Revolutionary documents of all time: the Declaration of the Rights of Man and of the Citizen.

Containing just 17 short articles, the first being that "Men are born and remain free and equal in rights," the Declaration proclaimed the death of the old order with its division of society into three separate and unequal estates. They replaced the old divine right of kings with the solemn declaration that, "sovereignty resides essentially in the nation. No body nor individual may exercise any authority which does not proceed directly from the nation." Considering that the Assembly represented the national will, the King's authority was therefore rendered subordinate to theirs. Clever, no?

The document protected certain individual rights spelled out in both the United States Constitution (less than a year old at that point) and the Bill of Rights, which was still awaiting ratification in 1789. It prohibited *ex post facto* laws and bills of attainder, guaranteed equal protection and due process of the law, provided for the separation of powers, and forbad seizure of private property except for public purposes and after providing just compensation (i.e., eminent domain). After a lengthy fight by the clerical members of the Assembly, it even guaranteed freedom of speech, the press, and of religion, with the proviso that they shall not "disturb the public order" and that people will be "responsible for such abuses of this freedom."

There was far more disagreement over exactly what form the newly created French State would take. What would the role of the king be? Would the legislature be unicameral or bicameral? How would elections take place and who could vote? Lafayette proposed a legislature containing both an upper and a lower house, with the king exercising essentially the same powers as the newly created office of President of the United States.

While conservatives supported these ideas, the bulk of the former Third Estate representatives opposed them. After fighting so hard against dividing the legislature up by order, they were not prepared to agree to an upper, and no doubt noble-dominated, house. No, just as the Nation is one and indivisible, so too must there only be one legislative body. The National Assembly voted down the upper house overwhelmingly on September 10; the New France would have a unicameral legislature, known as the Legislative Assembly.

The issue of the King's role was an even thornier subject. Louis had been dragging his feet over granting royal assent to the August Decrees and the Declaration of Rights, increasing suspicion about his commitment to these changes. A small but vocal minority, such as Sieyès and a young unknown lawyer from Arras named Maximilien de Robespierre, argued that the King should have a ceremonial role only with no veto power. Ultimately, the deputies reached a compromise where the King would retain a 'suspensive' veto, meaning that he could delay legislation but not stop it entirely. That provision also passed with strong support on September 15.

Perhaps the most radical provision in the new constitution was the abolition of the old French provinces. To the delegates, these provinces with their strange shapes, varying laws, and special privileges were an affront to reason. Taking their place would be 83 departments, rationally divided so that all were roughly uniform in size and population. To distance themselves further from their provincial past, the departments took their names from local geographic features – rivers, mountain ranges and such. By necessity, provincial government went out the window. The royal *intendants* were gone, replaced by departmental *préfets*. The regional parlements and private courts, long bastions of noble power, were likewise abolished and replaced by a uniform independent judiciary.

The business of completing the constitution dragged on for some time – all the way until 1791 in fact, giving it the unofficial (and none too creative) title, the Constitution of 1791. While the document was extremely progressive for its time, it fell far short in its professed commitment to equality. When the delegates talked about the rights of "Man" they really did just mean men, and more specifically white men. Women would have the same rights in the New France as they did in the Old France – none. Olympe de Gouges, an influential female playwright and political pamphleteer who

championed such radical causes as the abolition of slavery, the end of capital punishment, the right to divorce, and the decriminalization of pre-marital sex, produced her own Declaration of the Rights of Woman and the Female Citizen, calling for full gender equality. The Assembly thoroughly ignored it. Similarly, the status of slavery in France's Caribbean colonies was kept extremely ambiguous in the new constitution, as were the rights of free blacks. This confusion led to slave uprisings in France's wealthiest colony of Saint-Domingue. Led by Toussaint L'Ouverture and Jean-Jacques Dessalines, this uprising eventually led to the first successful slave rebellion in the New World, ending French colonial rule and establishing the independent state of Haiti.

Not even all white men had the franchise under the Constitution of 1791. Only 'active' citizens could vote, and they were limited to taxpaying males over the age of 25. Even amongst the active citizens, only the most active were eligible for election, and were defined as belonging to the top 10% in income. This made the new electoral system paradoxically more unequal than the Estates-General. Camille Desmoulins, consummate grenade-tosser that he was, publicly denounced this distinction of citizens based on wealth declaring that the truly 'active' citizens were the ones who stormed the Bastille.

Meanwhile, as the Assembly remade the country in their own image, the King and his ministers grew increasingly concerned. Not wanting to make the same mistake of calling in foreign mercenaries to safeguard the palace, the King summoned one of the most elite units in the French army to Versailles – the dreaded Flanders Regiment. During the customary welcoming party, the troops feasted lavishly and rowdily toasted the royal family, who made a brief courtesy appearance. When word of this reached Jean-Paul Marat, writer of the most influential radical newspaper in Paris, *L'Ami du Peuple* (The Friend of the People), he couldn't resist letting such a juicy story go to waste. Expounding on the idea of the troops gorging themselves on fine food and wine while Paris starved, Marat also spread the rumor (possibly true, but likely embellished) that they ritually trampled on the tricolor cockade and swore insults against the Nation.

Word spread rapidly among the agitated masses of Paris. On the morning of October 5, a severe bread shortage caused a riot by a group of marketplace women. The riot quickly spread throughout the city as starving women converged on the Hôtel de Ville, demanding bread and weapons. Newly armed with cannon and muskets, they marched on Versailles to press their demands directly to the King and his hated foreign Queen. By the time evening came, nearly 10,000 armed and angry women had surrounded the palace, trapping the royal family inside.

Only the arrival of Lafayette and several thousand National Guardsmen were able to stop a wholesale slaughter. The crowd refused to disperse unless the King and Queen agreed to return with them to Paris. On the morning of October 6, Louis XVI agreed to go with them and reside at the Tuileries Palace in Paris; neither he nor his family would ever see Versailles again.

If there had been any question that the King's power was completely gone prior to these 'October Days,' his forced relocation to Paris by a mob of angry women answered it. From this point on, Louis XVI and Marie Antoinette were effectively prisoners in their own home. The National Assembly would relocate to Paris later that week as well, kept under the watchful eye of a Parisian mob who increasingly saw themselves as the guardians of the new Revolution.

Amidst all the constitution writing and dodging of enraged, pitch-fork-bearing washerwomen, the deputies to the National Assembly still had France's crushing debt crisis to resolve. The deputies realized that public confidence in them as a governing institution hinged on getting this right. The Assembly had continued to rack up enormous bills while it sat, none bigger than providing compensation for the multitude of offices and feudal privileges they abolished, but simply refusing to pay was out of the question. Mirabeau went so far as to call the debt a "national treasure" that must be protected at all costs. Chaos in the countryside meant that tax receipts were way down and even Necker was having trouble securing enough in loans to keep the government operating. They needed a new source of revenue that would raise a lot of money and fast. The solution the deputies settled on would be the most radical act of the young Revolution to date and the first to cause severe divisions in French society – they would nationalize the lands of the Church.

Originally proposed by Bishop Talleyrand (himself less than a model of priestly piety), he argued that the abolition of the clergy as a separate or-der and the end of feudalism meant that the former First Estate's extensive landholdings should be placed at the disposal of the Nation. The newly confiscated property could then be used to both pay down the national debt and allow the State to assume the social service functions formerly performed by the clergy. On November 2, 1789, the Assembly voted in favor of Talleyrand's proposal transforming all Church lands throughout the Kingdom into the *Biens Nationaux,* the National Property.

Of course putting so much land on sale all at once would have flooded the market and destroyed its value. Instead, Necker proposed that they issue bonds redeemable for national lands in order to monetize the property quickly. Originally floated in late December of 1789, these bonds, known as *assignats,* quickly circulated throughout the country and were exchanged as a form of paper currency. By April of next year, the Assembly formally

designated the *assignat* as legal tender. The delegates quickly fell in love with the *assignat* as the cure for all the country's financial ills and printed them by the boatload. While the original plan was to circulate 80 million *livres* worth of notes in 1790, before the year was out that number had already ballooned to 1.2 billion. This was far more than the value of the property supposedly backing it and predictably led to rapid inflation. As legal tender, the *assignat* could be used to pay all debts both public and private, turning Revolutionary France into a debtor's paradise. By the time the new Legislative Assembly finally took office in 1792, the *assignat* was only worth 50% of its par value and dropping. Necker, who opposed the runaway printing from the beginning, resigned his office in protest in September of 1790, and returned to his native Switzerland.

While the State now had the lands of the Church at its disposal, it also took on new obligations. It was now the government's job to pay the salaries of priests, run the hospitals, maintain the orphanages and schools, and provide relief to the poor. This was exactly what many of the progressive delegates had in mind all along. Just as they were modernizing, rationalizing, and democratizing (in theory) the machinery of government, so too must the same thing happen to the Church. There was no place in the New France for monks and nuns to idle away the hours singing Latin chants in their dusty abbeys and convents while the peasants labored for their daily bread. Accordingly, the Assembly abolished all monastic orders on February 13, 1790. On July 12, 1790, the reformers went a step further when they won approval for the Civil Constitution of the Clergy – officially turning the French Catholic Church into an arm of the State.

The first thing the Civil Constitution of the Clergy did was abolish the old dioceses. Like the rest of Catholic Europe, France was divided up into a number of dioceses each headed by a bishop. Much like the old heterogeneous hodgepodge of provinces, the dioceses sprang up by organic historical patterns and had no rational order. The southern part of the country had nearly twice the number of bishoprics as the northern part simply because it was Christianized first. The Civil Constitution made the new dioceses coterminous with the new departments, so that each one contained exactly one bishop. Even more radical, both the bishop and the parish priests were to be elected by their parishioners, not appointed by the Pope. While nominally recognized as the spiritual head of the Church and supreme in matters of religious doctrine, the Pope would have nothing more to do with Church operations in the country and only retained the right to be informed of election results. Furthermore, all clergymen, considering that they were now State employees, would be required to take a loyalty oath if they wished to keep their jobs.

The reaction was immediate and severe. The Archbishops of Aix and Clermont, both delegates to the National Assembly, staged a walkout in protest. Pope Pius VI condemned the document and urged Louis XVI not to ratify it (who predictably dragged his feet yet again). When only seven of France's 130 bishops took the oath, followed by about a third of parish priests, the schism was complete. The Church in France was now divided between oath-taking priests known as the constitutional or juroring clergy (from the opening line of the oath *"Je jure,"* French for "I swear") and the non-juroring or refractory clergy.

Up until this point, nearly all of the Assembly's actions had been broadly popular. Granted, it's not hard to have high favorability ratings when you end arbitrary arrests, guarantee freedom of speech, and tell people that they no longer need to provide free labor to their absentee landlord. This was the first time the Assembly took an action that alienated a large swath of the population. While most people wanted to see an end to clerical abuses, France was still a deeply Catholic country, especially in the more rural areas. The schism caused by the Civil Constitution of the Clergy forced ordinary people to choose between adherence to the Revolution and loyalty to their faith. It also served to fuel increasing political polarization on all sides.

The early days of consensus in the Assembly broke down and political factions began to emerge, with fault lines strikingly familiar to us today. Conservatives, on their heels since the first days of the Estates-General, were finally able to regain their footing by using the Civil Constitution of the Clergy to portray their progressive opponents as enemies of traditional faith and morals. Liberals saw the widespread refusal to take the oath as a sign that the clergy were hostile to reforms and that their conservative apologists wished to return to the bad old days of the *ancien régime*. The country divided geographically with conservatives stronger in the more rural southern and western parts of the country, while liberals had their power base in the urbanized north and east, particularly Paris. Even our concept of left-wing/right-wing politics comes from this period, as the conservative Monarchists sat on the right side of the Assembly hall, the moderate Royalist Democrats in the center, and the liberal National Party to the left.

HATRED OF
MARIE ANTOINETTE

As popular discontent with the Bourbon monarchy grew, more and more anger fell on the person of Marie Antoinette. The "Austrian Whore" was easy to caricature as an aloof, profligate, overly sexualized epicurean who cared nothing for her people; and was a regular object of ridicule in the *libelles* (the thoroughly libelous tabloids of their day). We know that she never actually said the most famous quote attributed to her, "Let them eat cake," nor did she conspire with a prostitute to seduce a cardinal into fraudulently obtaining an obscenely expensive diamond necklace (the infamous Diamond Necklace Affair), but somehow these depictions stuck. The reality is that Marie-Antoinette was both a caring queen and a rather independent-minded, even progressive woman. She enjoyed gambling, hunting, and reading about science and history. As a retreat from the suffocating formality of courtly life, she had a peasant hamlet built for her on the outskirts of Versailles where she could dress up *à la paysanne*. She was so fond of it that she even had her court-painter, the already controversial Louise Élisabeth Vigée-Le Brun (who shocked the art world by painting herself with an open-mouthed smile) depict her wearing peasant clothes in a portrait. Rather than endearing Marie to her people, the *Hameau de la Reine* only angered them more and came off as phony and patronizing. It seems that the only real sympathy she evoked was during her trial in front of the Revolutionary Tribunal. When asked for her response to the trumped up charges of incest with her eight-year-old son, the former queen stood silent. Only when one of the judges announced that he would take her silence as an admission did she say, "If I have not replied, it is because Nature itself refuses to respond to such a charge laid against a mother," winning her the admiration of the crowd. Regardless, Marie was executed two days later and her body unceremoniously tossed into an unmarked grave.

VII

A ROYAL PAIN: THE FLIGHT TO VARENNES

AND THE LEGISLATIVE ASSEMBLY

Throughout 1790 and into 1791, the Assembly continued its work of transforming the nation while the constitution slowly took shape. Robespierre passed a decree that forbid any members of the National Assembly from sitting on the new Legislative Assembly when it finally met (the so-called 'Self-Denying Ordinance'), so few delegates were tempted to wrap up quickly. In celebration of the one-year anniversary of the fall of the Bastille, they held a great public festival on the Champ de Mars with Talleyrand officiating over a patriotic high mass at the new Altar of the Nation.

Both Lafayette and King Louis XVI swore public oaths to preserve, protect, and defend the constitution. Not wishing to let this opportunity pass them by, the liberal members of the Assembly issued a decree banning all symbols and regalia associated with the *ancien régime,* including titles of nobility, coats of arms, and orders of chivalry. This punitive law only served to swell the ranks of the *émigrés,* as disgruntled nobles fled the country

to their less hostile neighbors. On the other side of the Alps in the city of Turin, the King's brothers, the Counts of Artois and Provence, had set up a court-in-exile, attracting *émigrés* and attempting to recruit foreign powers to their cause. They urged Louis to flee the country for his own safety and return at the head of an army to crush the Revolution. Louis ignored their letters and waited, believing that the changes were just about over and calm would soon return.

While perhaps a little naïve, the King was not entirely out of his mind to have thought this. A growing number of deputies in the Assembly believed that the Revolution had accomplished its core goals and should now devote itself to consolidating its gains. Both Mirabeau and Lafayette (who generally hated each other) agreed that if things continued to move too far too fast, the Revolution would unravel into bloody anarchy. Their shared objective was a liberal constitutional monarchy in France; the increasing influence of the radical deputies in the Assembly and casual acceptance of street violence by the Parisian mob alarmed them. While they had upended the old order, that did not mean they thought all order should go by the wayside – although it seemed only their outsized influence was holding together a center that wanted more than anything to rip itself apart.

The first tear came on April 2, 1791, when Mirabeau, renowned for his overindulgence in food, drink, and sex, died of a massive heart attack. With the great 'Torch of Provence' dead, his once formidable centrist coalition in the Assembly died with him. The royal family also lost one of their greatest defenders, having held their powdered noses long enough buy Mirabeau's support through a sizeable donation in 1790. Left with no friends in the Assembly, when the Paris Commune denied their request to vacation for the weekend at their country home of Saint-Cloud, Louis XVI and Marie Antoinette realized that they were completely isolated in the middle of a hostile city. It was as if a lightning bolt struck the aloof king and he finally awoke to the reality of the situation. He resolved to flee the country with his family, leaving behind a manifesto containing a list of grievances against the illegitimate Revolution and disassociating himself from any involvement with it, claiming that all his actions since the fall of the Bastille had been made under duress.

On the warm summer night of June 20, the royal family made their escape. Dressed up as common folk, they raced for the border with the Netherlands, then under the control of Marie's brother, the Emperor of Austria. After travelling all night and the next day, the local postmaster, Jean-Baptiste Drouet, spotted the King in the town of Sainte-Menehould – allegedly from seeing Louis' face on his money. Drouet, in Paul Revere style, rode ahead to the next town and alerted the local militia. There, in the sleepy village of Varennes, the royal family was placed under arrest less than thirty miles from the Dutch border. It would be the last time any of them would experience freedom ever again. On June 22, National Guardsmen arrived to bring them back to Paris where they would be kept under constant surveillance.

The "Flight to Varennes," as it became known, was pivotal in turning public opinion against the institution of the monarchy. Republicanism, once an ideology limited to the radical Cordeliers and Jacobin political clubs, was now discussed openly on the streets and in the coffee houses of Paris. Louis had betrayed the Revolution by fleeing from his own country. Even worse, the man might have gathered foreign armies to invade France and slaughter his own people. The thought of him acting as a faithful constitutional monarch under a new regime was no longer credible. Lafayette and his backers in the Assembly spread the fiction that the royal family had been kidnapped by extremists who sought to smuggle them out of the country. For their safety, the royal family would be kept under constant guard and his executive functions as king suspended pending a full investigation. For the first time in over 1,000 years, France was left without a governing monarch.

To the growing number of republicans in the Assembly, this was not enough. Increasing violence characterized June and July as radical political pamphlets urged the abolition of the monarchy. The conservatives in the Assembly knew that deposing the King would throw the entire country into chaos and necessitate they scrap their nearly complete constitution. On July 15, the Assembly voted to exonerate Louis from any blame in the Flight. The republicans were outraged and Jacques-Pierre Brissot, writer and editor-in-chief of the republican newspaper *Le Patriote Français* (The French Patriot), drafted a public petition demanding the King's removal from office as a traitor to the Nation. All those in favor of the petition were to assemble at the Altar of the Nation on the Champ de Mars to sign on July 17. By midday on the 17th, over 10,000 people had gathered on the Champ de Mars to sign the petition. Mayor Bailly, fearing he might have a riot on his hands, declared martial law and called in Lafayette to control the situation.

The Marquis de Lafayette appeared in person at the Champ de Mars with several hundred National Guardsmen, believing that his presence alone would defuse the tense situation. At first it seemed to work and the crowd began to disperse, until the agitators of the Bastille spoke out. Georges Danton and Camille Desmoulins rallied the crowd, denouncing Lafayette as a recalcitrant aristocrat, in the pocket of the royal court and a traitor to the nation. The two men shared a deep dislike for Lafayette – seeing him as an elitist, glory-seeking, wannabe George Washington – but they also recognized his considerable influence as a political rival. If they could destroy his reputation, the monarchy would be left without any popular defenders.

Responding to their speeches, the crowd hurled insults at Lafayette and began pelting the National Guardsmen with stones. The General realized he was losing control of a rapidly escalating situation and ordered his men to fire a warning shot over the heads of the rioters. Rather than frighten the rioters, they began to surge towards the troops. Fearing that the mob would overrun his men, Lafayette ordered that they fire directly into the crowd. Several dozen people died and many more were injured. While the crowd quickly broke and fled in all directions, the radical newspapers and political clubs now had the ammunition they needed to take down Lafayette, tarnishing his image forever as the perpetrator of the "Champ de Mars Massacre."

As France continued to unravel, foreign powers became more concerned about the Revolution spilling over into their borders. While France's traditional rivals in England, Prussia, and Austria might have enjoyed seeing

Louis eat a big slice of humble pie in 1789, all of them realized the growing danger the Revolution presented to their own reigns by 1791. Marie Antoinette had been sending regular correspondence to her brother, Emperor Leopold II of Austria, pleading with him to save her and her family. The *émigré* nobles, and most especially the King's brothers, used their money and influence to encourage foreign intervention in France. On August 27, 1791, Leopold II and Frederick William II, King of Prussia, issued the joint Declaration of Pillnitz, warning that they would take "all necessary measures" to protect the royal family if they were threatened. While vaguely worded and essentially an empty threat, the Declaration gave credence to the republicans' claim. What other proof did they need that the already-suspect King and Queen were engaged in an international conspiracy to further the cause of royal tyranny? Paranoia ran rampant and the Assembly passed stricter laws against *émigrés*, refractory priests, and all others seen as supporting the old regime and its foreign backers. When the Constitution of 1791 finally limped across the finish line on September 13, the Assembly had fractured into hostile factions, the King's loyalty was in doubt, and the threat of war loomed on the horizon. The experiment in constitutional monarchy was effectively over before it even began.

VIII

THE CENTER CANNOT HOLD:
THE LEGISLATIVE ASSEMBLY TO
THE NATIONAL CONVENTION

Their work complete, the National Assembly voted to dissolve itself on September 30, and the newly constituted Legislative Assembly was sworn in on October 1. Due to the Self-Denying Ordinance championed by Robespierre, none of the delegates to the National Assembly were eligible to sit on the Legislative Assembly. The result was exactly what the crafty politician had intended all along. The radical Jacobin and Cordeliers clubs campaigned hard for their candidates during the elections and the results paid off. As a whole, the members of the new Legislative Assembly were far younger (half the deputies were under the age of 30) and more liberal than those in the National Assembly. Gone were nearly all the priests and nobles with their seats going to attorneys and political writers. The ideological shift was immediately noticeable. Of the 745 members, only 165 sat on the right as members of the moderately conservative Feuillants (constitutional monarchists). The left contained double the number of members, divided between the Girondins (moderate republicans) and

Jacobins (radical republicans). The remaining 220 members were independents or unaffiliated and sat in the middle of the Assembly.

Conflict arose immediately between the Crown and the Assembly when their first acts in office were to pass new laws confiscating the property of *émigrés,* condemning them to death if they did not return by the New Year, and voiding the pensions of refractory priests. Louis XVI vetoed these measures as unduly harsh, which again caused the Assembly to question his commitment to the Revolution. Less than a month into the new constitutional government, the King and the Assembly were at war with each other. But it was war with Austria that both increasingly desired.

Brissot, the pamphleteer responsible for the Champ de Mars Massacre and Girondin leader in the Assembly, became the most prominent proponent of war. Brissot and his supporters believed that war would unite the nation against a common enemy while simultaneously spreading the Revolution abroad. They believed victory would come easily as France's long-oppressed neighbors welcomed her troops with open arms as liberators. Louis also desired war, but for completely different reasons. He knew the army was in complete disarray. The vast majority of the aristocratic officer corps had emigrated, leaving the troops without effective leadership. As for the troops themselves, many had deserted their posts due to lack of pay. Discipline had completely broken down in most camps and the men were divided in their loyalties between the Crown and the Assembly. Surely, the well-trained professional armies of Austria and Prussia would crush the weak French forces and the Revolution would collapse. Robespierre, now head of the Jacobin club, saw this danger and became the vocal leader of the doves. Still, the drumbeat of war proved too great for even Robespierre to hold back. On April 20, 1792, after hearing of troop mobilizations along France's eastern border, Louis XVI appeared in the hall of the Legislative Assembly and asked for a declaration of war against Austria. The measure passed by a landslide with only seven members voting nay.

With war declared, Revolutionary France was now literally committed to a fight for its life. As the armies fought abroad, the revolutionaries turned their attention to weeding out domestic enemies. Although Robespierre's attempt to abolish the death penalty met with failure, the Assembly agreed that they needed a more humane form of execution for a more enlightened time. Under the old regime, different methods of execution were prescribed for different people. Nobles were entitled to a private beheading and had the privilege of hiring their own executioner. Commoners were simply hanged for most offenses and could be subjected to far crueler forms of execution – drawing and quartering, breaking on the wheel, burning at the stake – depending on the offense. First proposed to the National Assembly by Dr. Guillotin, the Legislative Assembly approved the use of his device (which he did not actually invent) for all executions on March 23, 1792. One month later, an average murderer, thief, and rapist by the name of Nicolas Pelletier became first to lose his head to this new device – the guillotine.

Meanwhile, during the spring and summer of 1792, the French armies invaded the Austrian Netherlands and made a complete hash of it. In one of the first battles near Lille, the French troops broke and ran at the first sight of the Austrians, murdering their general after he attempted to rally them. Things hardly improved over the following months as the depleted and disorganized armies suffered defeat after defeat. The Duke of Brunswick, supreme commander of the Austrian and Prussian allied armies, saw that the French were on the ropes and prepared to deliver his knockout blow. On August 1, he mobilized a large force, consisting of entire units of émigrés, and crossed the Rhine River, invading France itself. On the same day, he released a document known as the Brunswick Manifesto to wage psychological warfare on the civilian population. In the Manifesto, the Duke declared that France had lost and that his armies would soon occupy Paris. He warned that if the royal family were harmed in any way, he would unleash his troops on a killing spree and burn the historic city to the ground.

Much like the Declaration of Pillnitz, the Brunswick Manifesto backfired. Rather than scare the population into submission, it rallied them behind the revolutionary cause. It also sealed Louis' fate. For the second time, a foreign enemy championed the cause of the King by threatening the French people with violence. It's difficult to imagine how pervasive the atmosphere of fear and paranoia must have been in the capital at this time. French forces were in full retreat everywhere and German units had crossed the Rhine to march on Paris. Should they reach it, which seemed likely, the Revolution would die a bloody death and all of its supporters with it.

As the threat of violence grew, the revolutionaries looked to arm themselves. The working-class urban partisans organized themselves as the *sans-culottes,* referring to the fact that they wore the trousers of a laborer rather than the knee-britches (culottes) of the bourgeoisie. In the years to follow, the *sans-culottes* would become the frontline soldiers and self-appointed guardians of the Revolution. The composition of the National Guard too was changing. Traditionally middle class, moderately conservative, and loyal to Lafayette, the revolutionaries began organizing their own rival National Guard units in the provinces, known as the *fédérés.* While technically barred from entering Paris, several thousand of them were present by August to maintain order as all the other troops had gone to the front.

SANS CULOTTES

On the night of August 9, the revolutionaries made their move to overthrow the government in a violent *coup d'état*. Led once again by Danton and Desmoulins, a group of armed *fédérés* and *sans-culottes* first stormed the Hôtel de Ville, overthrowing the Paris Commune (once radical, but now viewed as too pliant and conservative) and installing a new 'Insurrectionary' Paris Commune. They wasted no time and proceeded to march directly on the Tuileries palace where the royal family was residing. More and more National Guard units deserted their posts and joined them on the way, swelling their numbers to nearly 20,000. When word reached the King of this imposing force en route, he decided to flee the palace with his family and make their way to the hall of the Legislative Assembly where he could ask for their protection. The 900 or so Swiss Guards tasked with defending the Tuileries put up a determined fight when the revolutionary force arrived, but they were ultimately overwhelmed and butchered to a man.

When the King and his family arrived at the hall of the Legislative Assembly they were forced to wait in the nearby reporter's box as the deputies debated their fate. With the mob now converging on the hall, the Assembly realized they needed a bold declaration to prevent more bloodshed – particularly their own! The crowd would not be pacified if Louis remained on the throne, yet the Assembly's own authority was based on the royalist constitution of 1791. Clearly, the government had fallen and a new constitution was needed. That very morning, the delegates passed a motion suspending the King from office and summoning a National Convention to meet in Paris for the purposes of drafting a new constitution. The royal family was taken into custody and confined in the Temple of Paris; the monarchy was finished.

Prior to August 10, the moderate constitutional monarchists were dominant while the republicans occupied a radical fringe. The storming of the Tuileries and fall of the Legislative Assembly changed all that. Not only were the monarchists now designated as enemies of the State, but all pretext of legality went by the wayside. Until the National Convention formally convened on September 20, France was in a state of complete anarchy. The Insurrectionary Paris Commune had taken control of the reins of government and those in power enforced their will through *sans-culottes* muscle. They dictated to the remnants of the Assembly for the next six weeks and assigned their own people to all manner of posts – even Danton got a new job as Minister of Justice. When La-

fayette (then commanding a French army on the Dutch border) received word of his dismissal on August 19, he attempted to rally the troops and march on Paris to overthrow the usurpers. His own men declined to follow him. The former war hero who had worked so hard to turn France into a constitutional monarchy refused to serve an illegitimate government. He crossed the border and turned himself over to the enemy, where he would remain a POW in Austrian captivity for the next five years. Lafayette's family only escaped retribution through the efforts of the American foreign office to smuggle them out of the country.

In early September, the Duke of Brunswick's forces captured the seemingly impregnable fortresses of Longwy and Verdun. Panic gripped the

Parisian population once again as the enemy was now quite literally at the gates. Afraid for their lives and sick of defeat, the revolutionaries blamed disloyal elements at home for the dismal war effort. Whipped into a frenzy by the bloodthirsty Marat, the *sans-culottes* took it upon themselves to weed out these disloyal elements, root and stem, by massacring all those they deemed Enemies of the People. Refractory priests, supporters of the monarchy, former nobles, and even regular prisoners in the wrong place at the wrong time were all indiscriminately murdered. By the end of the month, nearly 1,500 people lay dead from the "September Massacres."

Quite satisfied that their domestic enemies either were all either dead or had fled the country, the rowdy *sans-culottes* began to enlist in enormous numbers to throw the invaders out of their homeland. As they marched to the front, they loudly sang the newest and most popular patriotic song, *La Marseillaise*. First introduced to the crowds of Paris by *fédérés* from Marseilles, the song called on the people to resist the foreign tyrants who had come to kill their families and place the nation in bondage once again. The defiant, militaristic tune replaced the more laid-back *Ça Ira* ("It'll be fine") as the preferred hymn of the revolutionaries.

On September 20, 1792, the new National Convention convened in Paris for the purposes of drafting a constitution to replace the defunct Constitution of 1791. For the first time, all male citizens over the age of 21 were eligible to vote. By a stroke of unimaginable luck, September 20 also happened to be the day the French army won its first major victory at the Battle of Valmy. Reinforced by the fanatic *sans-culottes* and inspired with revolutionary zeal, the army halted the Duke of Brunswick's advance on Paris and made the Prussians – never all that excited about supporting their rival Austrians anyway – bow out of the war. Paris erupted in elation when they realized they wouldn't be slaughtered after all, and the National Convention seized the initiative by voting to abolish the monarchy the very next day. On September 22, 1792, at 12:01 a.m., France officially became a republic for the first time.

DR. GUILLOTIN'S MONSTER

While it was actually invented by Dr. Antoine Louis, the guillotine took its name from Dr. Joseph-Ignace Guillotin, a French physician and member of the National Assembly who recommended its usage during a debate on capital punishment reform in 1789. Originally elected to the Estates-General as a Third Estate representative, Dr. Guillotin was a medical reformer and a social justice advocate. Prior to the Revolution, he had a successful private practice in Paris and spent his free time teaching at the university and providing free treatment to the poor. While in the National Assembly, he chaired a committee that surveyed hospitals, asylums, orphanages, and old age homes, and initiated the first steps toward regulation of the medical profession. Much like Robespierre, Dr. Guillotin was personally opposed to the death penalty but realized that outright abolition was unlikely. Instead, he wished to rationalize the process by making it as quick and painless as possible while eliminating class distinctions in the form of punishment. While he championed Dr. Louis's device as a means to achieve this, the machine became associated forever with Dr. Guillotin after he unartfully declared to the Assembly, "Now, with my machine, I cut off your head in the twinkling of an eye, and you would never even feel it." The line became a popular joke throughout Paris and was reprinted in several newspapers. While he would become one of the first French physicians to support Dr. Edward Jenner's practice of vaccination and was a founding member of the Paris Faculty of Medicine (later the National Academy of Medicine), he could never shake his association with the device that far outlived both him and his family (who later changed their name out of embarrassment). The guillotine would remain France's only official form of execution until the abolition of the death penalty in 1981.

IX

VIVE LA RÉPUBLIQUE!

Unlike the Legislative Assembly, largely composed of unknown amateurs, the deputies to the National Convention formed a veritable all-star team of the biggest names in the Revolution: Robespierre, Danton, Marat, Desmoulins, Brissot, Pétion, the Duke of Orléans (now known by his new revolutionary name Philippe Égalité), and even Thomas Paine of *Common Sense* fame. Over the next three years, the National Convention would act as the supreme executive, legislative, judicial, and constitution-drafting body for the entire French Republic.

The Convention's first order of business was to deal with the 10-ton crowned elephant in the room, the fate of Louis XVI. Sure, you can abolish a kingdom, but what exactly do you do with an ex-king? The simmering tensions between the former allies of the moderate Girondins and radical Jacobins finally boiled over into direct conflict over this issue. The Jacobins were strongly in favor of trying Louis XVI for high treason. The twenty-five year old firebrand, Saint-Just, argued that they should execute Louis without trial, as the very act of creating the Republic rendered the judgment of guilty. The Girondins feared that trying and executing the former king would only lead to more instability and perhaps even civil war; the best course of action was simply to leave him in prison and go about the nation's business. What ultimately sealed the King's fate was the discovery of a lock box containing his damning personal correspondence with royalist sympathizers at home and abroad. The issue was decided: Louis would face trial in front of the National Convention.

On December 3, 1792, the Convention issued an indictment of the King, now addressed as Citizen Louis Capet (the last name taken from the Capetian dynasty of early French kings), containing thirty-three charges of treason against the nation. On December 11, the trial began with Louis hauled in front of the Convention to hear the charges read aloud to him. For the next two weeks Barère, the President of the Convention, acted as chief prosecutor, grilling the former monarch on his attempts to undermine the Revolution and collaborate with its enemies abroad. Louis assembled a crack defense team, headed by Raymond Desèze as lead counsel, one of the best lawyers in France. By all accounts, Desèze made a strong case for his client, with even Marat commending his skills as an advocate. Louis also made a powerful statement in his own defense, finally finding his voice and impressing some deputies by declaring his undying love for the people and nation, regardless of what happened to him. Going into deliberations the verdict was far from a fait accompli, and some members of the Jacobins feared that his spirited defense might have won him enough support to save his head.

For the next several weeks the Convention debated his fate. The question of guilt was never really in doubt. 693 delegates voted guilty, twenty-three abstained. Not a single vote was in favor of acquittal. The vote on the sentence was much closer. Robespierre, long a vocal opponent of capital punishment, made an exception in this case and declared, "the fatal truth: Louis must die so that the Nation may live." Even Philippe Égalité, Louis' own cousin, voted for death, perhaps to shore up his revolutionary cred and save his own neck (spoiler alert: it didn't work). On January 17, the Convention announced its sentence. Out of 721 total votes cast, 355 voted for either imprisonment, banishment, or death with a suspended sentence, while 361 voted for death without delay, narrowly passing by a mere six votes. The date for the King's execution was set for January 21, 1793.

At 10 a.m. that morning, Louis was taken by cart to the Place de la Révolution (now the Place de la Concorde, home of the famous Hôtel de Crillon and the United States Embassy). The non-juroring priest, Father Edgeworth, accompanied him up the scaffold and recorded Louis' last words to the hushed crowd of onlookers: "I die innocent of all the crimes laid to my charge; I pardon those who have occasioned my death; and I pray to God that the blood you are going to shed may never be visited on France." Before he could speak any further the drum roll began. Louis was strapped onto a board and slid firmly into place under the guillotine. At 10:22 the blade fell, and His Majesty Louis XVI, by the grace of God King of France and Navarre, was dead.

The execution of Louis XVI was perhaps the seminal event of the entire Revolution. What died on the guillotine that day was not just Louis the man, but the very institution of kingship he represented. What better way to express the sovereignty of the People over kings than to execute the monarch himself? For the revolutionaries, there was no going back from an act like this.

The safest Job in France

Charles Henri Sanson, The King's Executioner (in both senses of that)

Like Hernán Cortés burning his ships so that his men could not return home, the Jacobins knew that killing the King committed the nation to pursuing revolutionary republicanism at all costs. Peace was no longer an option; the great monarchial powers of Europe would never accept the legitimacy of a regicidal regime. France had now committed herself to a fight to the death that would last until Napoleon's final defeat at Waterloo in 1815. Twenty-three years of nearly constant war spanning the entirety of the European continent at the cost of millions of lives became one of the Revolution's most tragic legacies.

The King's execution not only turned the rest of Europe against France, but also divided the already fractured country even further against itself. As you may have noticed by now, most of the action has centered on Paris, but France is much bigger than just its capital city (contrary to the beliefs of many Parisians). The more rural, conservative parts of the country – which were pretty much everywhere outside the big cities of Paris, Lyons, Bordeaux, Marseilles, and Toulouse – had soured on the Revolution ever since the Civil Constitution of the Clergy in 1790. The execution of Louis XVI only agitated them even more, and that agitation turned into outright rebellion in 1793,

after the Convention decreed the first national military draft: the *levée en masse.*

In January of 1793, Spain and Portugal declared war on France. Then, in a hubristic act of epic proportions, the Convention declared war preemptively on Great Britain and Holland. "War on castles, peace for cottages," was the cry, as the very institution of monarchy itself became the enemy. The Convention declared that it was France's solemn duty as a liberated nation to export the Revolution abroad, providing aid to all those "seeking to recover their lost liberty." Of course if providing that aid resulted in the Republic acquiring some new lands at the expense of aristocrats, bishops, and kings, then it was all to the better!

Never before in the history of Europe was a country simultaneously at war with every single one of its neighbors. To confront this threat, the Convention would need more manpower than any power had been able to muster since the fall of the Roman Empire. In February, the Convention drafted 300,000 new recruits to reinforce the armies. In August, they went a step further, formally putting the entire nation on a war footing. "The young men shall fight; the married men shall forge arms and transport provisions; the women shall make tents and clothes and shall serve in the hospitals; the children shall turn old lint into linen; [and] the old men shall betake themselves to the public squares in order to arouse the courage of the warriors and preach hatred of kings and the unity of the Republic!" With this decree, the Revolution birthed the modern concept of the Nation-at-Arms. The all-in military mobilizations of the 20th century world wars were in a sense the children of the French Revolution. While the armies still lacked in experienced troops and officers, the sheer weight of French numbers was something the small, professional armies of the monarchial powers had never dealt with before. By the end of 1793, the Republic had nearly 700,000 citizens under arms, with the number rising to well over a million by 1794.

Then as now, forced military service was not a popular thing. While civil disturbances broke out across the country over the levy, northwestern France erupted into a bloody guerilla war that would last for three years and cost over 200,000 lives. Calling themselves the 'Catholic and Royal Army of the Vendée' (the department they originated in), the Vendéens refused to shed their blood for what they viewed as a radical, illegitimate, and impious government. After several cities fell to the Vendéen army, the Convention diverted nearly 50,000 troops to pacify the region. Going hand-in-hand with the new concept of total war, the Convention's generals instituted a scorched earth policy in the Vendée. Farms, forests, and villages were burned and people, woman and children included, were indiscriminately slaughtered. General Westermann, in correspondence back to Paris, declared that his extermination of the local population was so complete that "there is no more Vendée . . . mercy is not a revolutionary sentiment." General Carrier (perhaps the first person ever sentenced to death for war crimes) executed thousands of civilians in ritualized mass drownings. The military suppression of the revolt in the Vendée was so severe that there are still efforts to have it classified as a genocide in France today.

By April of 1793, the outlook for the Republic was bleak. The domestic situation was rapidly deteriorating as revolts spread throughout the provinces and the Parisian population rioted over bread shortages and rising prices. The greatest blow came on April 6, when General Dumouriez, the victor of Valmy and prominent supporter of the Girondin faction, defected to the Austrians. Imagine the panic of those in power – you are simultaneously fighting a losing battle against every other nation in Europe, your greatest general just went rogue and joined your enemies, a counter-revolution is sweeping through the countryside, and there are daily riots outside your window by a crowd that will literally tear you apart if they aren't appeased quickly.

This was the textbook definition of desperate times, and the Convention responded with desperate measures. As an emergency response to the crisis, they created the Committee of Public Safety. Composed of twelve delegates, eventually headed by Robespierre, the Committee was endowed with nearly unlimited powers to ensure the security of the Republic by any means necessary. In one of their first acts, they created a ruthlessly efficient tool to weed out internal dissidents, conspirators, and traitors: the Revolutionary Tribunal. A court solely dedicated to prosecuting political crimes, this body would condemn thousands of people to death by the guillotine as the Revolution turned into a national bloodletting.

In order to make their mark quickly, the Committee of Public Safety took it upon themselves to finish drafting the constitution, which they completed in only two months (the project had been lingering on since September 1792). This new Constitution of 1793 formed a manifesto of progressive ideas that was truly revolutionary in a way that the Constitution of 1791 was not. The new constitution extended several rights, such as granting the franchise to all citizens (but still only to males, it wasn't that ahead of its time), the presumption of innocence in criminal cases, trial by jury, the abolition of slavery, and unlimited freedom of speech, assembly, religion, and the press. Even more remarkable, it contained a number of social guarantees that all citizens of the Republic were entitled to, such as the right to a free public education, financial assistance in times of hardship, and a guarantee of full employment. It even recognized the right of insurrection when the government violates these rights.

Regrettably, the Constitution of 1793 never had a chance to go into effect and was destined to remain a list of lofty aspirations rather than a true governing document. Soon after ratification, the National Convention (originally assembled for the sole purpose of creating the new constitution, remember) declared that the constitution could not go into effect at present due to the existing state of "national emergency." The Convention would remain in power with the Committee of Public Safety running the country until the wars were over. They placed the Constitution of 1793 inside in a wooden box and hung it above the floor of the Convention, its guarantees of rights and freedoms literally suspended in air while the Committee below reigned with absolute authority.

Meanwhile, the political rivalry between the Girondins and Jacobins finally came to a head. The Girondins, once members of the radical left in the Legislative Assembly, were now the conservatives in the Convention. The key difference between the two factions was that the Jacobins favored centralizing power in Paris while the Girondins wanted to see more authority delegated to the regional departments. When in spring of 1793, several cities in southern France resisted the dictates of the Convention, the Jacobins quickly pinned the blame on the Girondins as "federalist" agitators. The Girondins did themselves no favors with the Parisian population by accusing the popular Jacobin fire-eater Marat of sedition before the Revolutionary Tribunal. After the Tribunal acquitted Marat of all charges, the jubilant crowd raised him on their shoulders and paraded him through the streets as he cried for the heads of his accusers. When the Girondin leader Maximin Isnard proclaimed that if the Convention continued to trample on the rights of the provinces then "France would march on Paris," the Jacobins finally had the pretext they needed to purge their political rivals from the Convention.

On May 26, Robespierre gave a stirring speech at the Jacobin club where he called on the people of Paris to eliminate the corruption that had seized the Convention and was putting the Revolution in peril. The radicalized Parisian *sans-culottes* and National Guard regiments got the message – they took up arms and surrounded the hall of the National Convention, demanding the arrest of the Girondin leaders. The terrified Convention acquiesced. The loss of their leadership shattered the Girondins and left the Jacobins in complete control of the government. For the next two years, France in effect would be a one-party state, under the not-so-benevolent dictatorship of Maximilien Robespierre and his Committee of Public Safety.

A REPUBLIC OF VIRTUE –

A REPUBLIC OF TERROR

The bookish, idealistic, and pacifistic Robespierre rose from insignificance in 1789, to the pinnacle of power in 1793, due to a quality few other revolutionaries possessed: he was a true believer. Known to his colleagues as "the Incorruptible," Robespierre had a reputation for extreme personal austerity and was a pathological workaholic. The man had no wife, no children, and actively shunned all material comforts. While it might be a stretch to say that Robespierre cultivated this image purely for PR purposes, he undoubtedly wished to portray himself as the ideal revolutionary – a kind of secular priest, married to the Republic itself. To Robespierre, the Republic was more than just a form of government, but rather the next step in human social evolution. His ideal republic was both forward looking – the ignorance and superstition of ages past replaced by a government based on reason – and backward looking – a return to the lost classical values of ancient Greece and Rome. This new form of government, which Robespierre called his "Republic of Virtue," would require new citizens as well. It was the job of the true revolutionary to create not only the new government, but also the New Man.

To establish a definitive break with the past, in October of 1793, the Convention voted to adopt a new Republican calendar. The old Gregorian calendar with its irrational assortment of days and months named after old gods and kings wasn't befitting this new modern era. The new calendar was decimally sublime: each month consisting of three, ten-day weeks, and each day consisting of ten, 100-minute hours. While it never quite caught on, the Committee of Public Education (far less feared than the Committee of Public Safety, at least to non-students) extended this principle to measurements of length, creating the forerunner of the modern metric system. Rather than date the year from the birth of Christ, henceforth the years would be dated from September 22, 1793, the day the Republic was proclaimed and history began anew. In keeping with the Enlightenment era reverence for nature, the months were given descriptive names like *Brumaire* ("fog" for October), *Ventôse* ("windy" for February), *Prairial* ("pasture" for May), and *Thermidor* ("heat" for July).

Part of the motivation behind the new calendar was to deinstitutionalize the role of the Catholic Church in French life. Things had been going downhill for the Church ever since the split over the Civil Constitution of the Clergy in 1790. As the Revolution grew more radicalized, people began to see the Church, with its monarchial pope and close alliance to archrival Austria, as a counter-revolutionary *agent provocateur* of the old regime. A new religion, dedicated to the principles of reason, equality, justice, liberty, and natural law was needed to replace superstitious and royalist Catholicism. A group of far-left ultra-revolutionaries known as the *enragés* ("the enraged ones," we'll see them again later) took up the cause and pursued a policy of dechristianization. Mobs roamed the countryside looting churches (the term *vandalism* arose during this period), smashing relics, beheading saints, and forcing priests to adjure their faith and marry on pain of death. They created a new religion, the Cult of Reason, to promote revolutionary ideology. Atheistic and civic-minded, this new religion promoted the worship of pure reason and celebrated festivals commemorating virtue, philosophy, and natural cycles to replace the old high holy days. They even transformed the famous Cathedral of Notre Dame into a Temple of Reason, and celebrated the first Festival of Reason on November 10, 1793. Soon after, the Convention officially banned all forms of Christian worship throughout the country. No church bell would ring again in France for another two years.

On August 28, 1793, a British fleet captured the port city of Toulon and destroyed France's entire Mediterranean fleet. Making matters worse, they were able to sail in unopposed after royalists took control of the city and let the British in. It was France's greatest military disaster to date and sent the Convention into a panic. Just one month prior, on July 13, a Girondin sympathizer by the name of Charlotte Corday entered Marat's room and stabbed him to death while he was in the bathtub.

PERFECT! DON'T MOVE A MUSCLE.

This act, combined with the ongoing revolts throughout the country, convinced the Committee of Public Safety that radical measures were needed to safeguard the Revolution from its enemies, both foreign and domestic. On September 17, they passed a decree known as the Law of Suspects. It established a secret police force of 'surveillance committees' and deputized them to arrest anyone who "showed themselves to be supporters of tyranny, of federalism, or to be enemies of liberty." This mushy standard meant that anyone viewed as being too 'aristocratic,' or even just insufficiently supportive of the Convention ran the risk of being hauled before the Revolutionary Tribunal. Enforcing this decree were the *sans-culottes,* increasingly the personal paramilitary force of Robespierre and the Committee of Public Safety. Until they could safely secure the Republic from the clutches of her enemies, Terror, the Committee famously declared, would be the order of the day. When the Terror finally ended nine months later, over 17,000 people had been left a head shorter under the merciless falling blade of the 'National Razor.'

This period, appropriately called the Reign of Terror, is perhaps the most well-known of the entire Revolution. Ironically, the quick, 'humane' (even clinical) death offered by the guillotine enabled the rapid execution of thousands of people in a way the old, more personal forms of execution under the old regime never could. The widowed former Queen, Marie Antoinette, became the Terror's first famous victim on October 16.

J.-L. David famously sketches "the Widow Capet" on her way to the scaffold.

Closely following her two weeks later was the Girondin leadership, arrested back in May. In November, Philippe Égalité, the former Duke of Orléans, followed his cousin Louis XVI to the scaffold. Bailly, the first revolutionary mayor of Paris under the Commune and former President of the National Assembly, long hated by the *sans-culottes* for his role in the Champ de Mars Massacre, went next. Many more would follow in 1794.

The foremost proponent of the Terror was the representative from the Aisne, Louis Antoine de Saint-Just, popularly called the 'Angel of Death.' Robespierre admired the young man's revolutionary zeal, and Saint-Just looked up to Robespierre as an idol. While the two developed a mentor-protégé relationship, Saint-Just was always the more extreme of the two and pushed Robespierre in that direction. Unlike Robespierre's vision of an Arcadian Republic of Virtue, Saint-Just modeled his ideal republic on ancient Sparta. In his fantasy world, the State would remove young boys from their mothers at age six and raise them to be warriors, statesmen, scholars, or laborers based on their merits. The State would hold all property in common and use it for the betterment of the Republic as a whole. He pursued these ideas in his notorious (and never fully implemented) Ventôse Decrees, which proposed the confiscation of all property held by *émigrés* and convicted traitors, with the State re-distributing them to true revolutionaries.

Saint Just

While Robespierre abhorred violence of any form, he believed that harsh measures were necessary to save the Republic. Saint-Just took a much more sanguine attitude towards killing and viewed the Terror as a kind of crucible – one that would remove the weaknesses and impurities from society, leaving behind a pure, hardened revolutionary alloy. Saint-Just saw no need to cloak violence in euphemism or Terror in high-minded justifications, but spoke plainly about his intent. Not only traitors deserved death according to Saint-Just, but also those who were merely indifferent, passive, or apathetic. Never one for understatement, he delivered famously grisly lines on the floor of the Convention such as, "a nation generates itself only upon heaps of corpses," and that "the vessel of the Revolution can only arrive safely in port on a sea reddened with torrents of blood." Saint-Just quickly developed a heated rivalry with old guard revolutionaries Danton and Desmoulins, viewing them as soft appeasers, while they saw him as a pompous, self-righteous upstart.

The Committee used the guillotine not only to weed out counter-revolutionaries (both real and imagined) but also as a tool of political oppression. With the Girondins dead or in hiding, the Jacobin faction was now supreme in both the Convention and Committee of Public Safety. As often happens in these situations, the once unified Jacobins split into an extremist faction, the *enragés* led by Hébert, and a moderate faction, the *indulgents* led by Danton.

Jacques Hébert was a political journalist who became wealthy and famous through his radical newspaper, *Le Père Duchesne*. Before the Revolution, most political papers were self-consciously highbrow and written for a bourgeois audience. In 1790, Hébert had the idea of making a newspaper that the everyday working man could relate to. He created a character named Père Duchesne, a vulgar, pipe-smoking, furnace maker, who could act as a mouthpiece for Hébert. The paper, with its coarse dialogue, dirty jokes, and violent rhetoric, quickly became a favorite of the *sans-culotte* crowd. When Hébert won a lucrative government contract to distribute his papers to the armies in 1792, he became an extremely rich and influential man. After

Marat's assassination in July of 1793, Hébert positioned himself to carry on the literary torch of extreme, radical revolution.

Politically to the left of the Jacobins, Hébert's *enragés* advocated for open class warfare and pressed for a sharply progressive income tax along with strong state controls over the economy. In part to appease the *enragés,* in September of 1793, the Convention passed a General Maximum (not to be confused with General Maximus) putting sharp price controls on food and other essentials. While intended to stop price gouging and allow people to buy necessities at rates they could afford, the hyperinflation of the *assignat* and low prices set in the Maximum meant that merchants actually would be taking a loss by selling these items. Predictably, merchants refused to stock the products or sold them on the black market, resulting in even more scarcity. The lack of food led to more demands by the *enragés* for the government to crack down on 'speculators' while hundreds of merchants were denounced as hoarders and forced to appear before the Revolutionary Tribunal.

Opposite the *enragés* were the *indulgents*, ironically led by the radicals of yesteryear, Georges Danton and Camille Desmoulins. It's generally a good indicator that a revolution has passed you by when your once far-left, progressive views become regarded as stodgy and conservative. While both men were principal agitators of the fall of the Bastille, the Champ de Mars massacre, and the assault on the Tuilieries, the purge of the Girondins soured them on the course the Revolution was taking. The Terror was becoming self-perpetuating as people denounced their neighbors to avoid being denounced themselves. The Committee of Public Safety had assumed total control over all aspects of government with Robespierre acting as virtual dictator. They realized that the Republic could not survive with constant war abroad and terrorism at home; France must make peace with her neighbors and dissolve the Committee to usher in normal, constitutional government. As a rebuke to the new blood who had hijacked their revolution, Desmoulins published a journal titled *Le Vieux Cordelier* ("The Old Cordelier," or "I was a Cordelier before it was cool"), wherein he rejected the *enragés* and called for an end to the Terror.

Lucile & Camille Desmoulins

In December of 1793, French forces succeeded in booting the British out of Toulon, thanks to the genius of a young Corsican artillery officer who only spoke French with a thick Italian accent and had the foreign-sounding name Napoleone Buonaparte. In recognition of his victory, the Convention promoted him to the rank of general and gave him command of an army. He would soon after assume the more French-sounding name history knows him by: Napoleon Bonaparte.

With the foreign situation under control once again, Robespierre could now consolidate his power going into 1794. The violent and disruptive ultra-revolutionary *enragés* were a constant thorn in his backside. As a serious and contemplative man, Robespierre despised Hébert and his tactics for making a mockery of his Republic of Virtue. While not religious himself, Robespierre believed in a Deist conception of a Supreme Being and understood the pragmatic value religion held in the lives of most people. Their attacks against religion were turning the countryside against the Convention and giving France's enemies easy propaganda to use against them. In yet another of the Revolution's countless ironies, the anti-death penalty Robespierre joined with his estranged *indulgent* friends, Danton and Desmoulins, to take down Hébert's faction Godfather-style.

Robespierre first used his influence to remove officials loyal to Hébert from office while Desmoulins attacked him in *Le Vieux Cordelier*, accusing him of corruption and accepting bribes from the British. Hébert saw the noose tightening around his neck; he would need to strike down Robespierre before it was too late. If he could rally the *sans-culottes* behind him, they would march on the Convention and demand the arrest of Robespierre, Danton, and Desmoulins just like they did to the Girondins the year prior. On March 6, 1794, Hébert called for an insurrection against the disloyal *indulgent* faction and the dictator Robespierre, yet few *sans-culotte* partisans joined his causes. Even the typically radical Paris Commune was strangely silent. Robespierre had played his hand perfectly by cowing potential opposition while simultaneously luring Hébert into declaring an open rebellion. Now the trap snapped shut. Saint-Just, Robespierre's right hand man in the Committee, denounced Hébert and his allies as traitors to the Nation. They were quickly arrested, tried before the Tribunal, and sent to the guillotine on March 24. Hébert, the man whose writings casually condemned so many others to death, reportedly fainted several times on his way up the scaffold.

With Père Duchesne's pipe permanently snuffed and the power of the *enragés* broken, the tireless crosshairs of the Committee fell next on its biggest critics, the *indulgent* faction of Danton and Desmoulins. The bloodthirsty Saint-Just, foremost proponent of the Terror, particularly hated the *indulgents* and sought to destroy them. Undeterred, Desmoulins openly rejected the policy of Terror and publicly urged his longtime friend Robespierre to turn his back on it. Danton, in characteristically brusque style, threatened that if any man called him a traitor he would rip his head off, "eat his brains and shit in his skull." Danton and Desmoulins were fiercely republican, but the increasingly violent course the Revolution was taking troubled them both deeply. They believed that their reputations and popular support would protect them from prosecution by the Tribunal while they pointed out the hypocrisy of the dictatorial Committee of Public Safety. However, their enemies were tenacious, and when word of a financial scandal broke, they pounced.

Rumors of corruption had swirled around Danton since before the Revolution. Unlike Robespierre, the true believer, and Desmoulins, the social liberal, Danton was a political opportunist, plain and simple. While all three men had careers as attorneys under the old regime, Robespierre and Desmoulins lived hand-to-mouth, representing helpless clients pro bono against powerful aristocratic and clerical interests. Danton, on the other hand, had a lucrative legal practice, even attaining the coveted position of King's Counsel. In many ways, Danton was the polar opposite of Robespierre. Unlike the small, academic, unassuming Maximilien, famously abstinent from fine food, drink, gambling and women, Danton was a huge, barrel-chested back slapper, well known throughout Paris for his equally massive appetites. To him, kickbacks were a just reward for being a Founding Father of the Republic. After all, what's so wrong about lining your own pockets while changing the world? While Danton was on top, nobody questioned his shady dealings.

However, once he started speaking out against the establishment, his enemies used their large dossier of corrupt financial dealings to attack him. Bribes, under the table payoffs, embezzlement from public funds – all these accusations, both truthful and not, came at Danton fast and furious. While he was able to shake off most of them, what ultimately brought him down was his involvement in a massive insider-trading scheme involving the French East India Company.

Danton

Originally founded as a publicly traded company in 1664, with a royal monopoly to import exotic goods and spices from the Far East, the French East India Company embodied all the royalist, preferential, and bourgeois aspects of the old regime the Jacobins hated most. In 1793, the Convention banned all joint-stock companies, forcing them to liquidate their assets under state supervision. The directors of the East India Company, hoping to cash out their stock for a tidy profit, paid off several members of the Convention to allow them to handle their own liquidation without government supervision. One of Danton's right hand men was a key player in this scheme, even forging official state documents in the process. The scandal was a huge embarrassment for the Convention, and while Danton's direct involvement was never proven, the implication alone (along with his reputation for greasy palms) was enough to call his loyalty into question.

With this evidence in hand, Saint-Just pushed ahead with his plans to arrest and try Danton and Desmoulins for crimes against the Republic. Robespierre, in a final attempt to save his friends from the guillotine, met with Danton for a private dinner, hoping to hash out their differences. While their relationship was always based more on mutual respect rather than warmth, and in truth the two men probably irritated each other to no end, the dinner went worse than expected. One of their exchanges, so memorable that Robespierre recorded it in his journal, perfectly describes the characters of both men to a tee. After urging Danton to recant his statements bashing the Committee of Public Safety and the Terror (which Danton refused, of course), an exasperated Robespierre said, "Well I suppose a man of your moral principles would not think that anyone deserved punishment." To which Danton sarcastically replied, "And I suppose you would be annoyed if none did!" This was the final break between Robespierre and the *indulgents;* he would no longer use his influence to protect them from prosecution. On March 30, at the urging of Saint-Just, the Committee issued warrants for the arrest of Danton, Desmoulins, and their associates. They would go before the very Revolutionary Tribunal they helped create in the first place.

Danton knew he had no hope of acquittal, so he decided to use this public stage to put the entire Revolution on trial. Freed from the need to censor his own speech, he appealed to the crowd in the courtroom, arguing that the Committee had become tyrannical and demanded that the Tribunal allow him to call witnesses in his defense (one of whom was Robespierre himself). His famous personal charm swayed the crowd once again, who cheered at every broadside he leveled at the regime. The public prosecutor, Antoine Quentin Fouquier-Tinville (who had only gotten the job thanks to a letter of recommendation written by his cousin, Desmoulins) feared that he was losing control of the courtroom. He asked the Committee for a special order, silencing the defendants and allowing the trial to proceed in their absence, which he received with Saint-Just's swift blessing. Amidst public outcry, he immediately wrapped up the nightmare of a trial and secured a quick conviction from the pliant jury. On that very same day, April 5, 1794, Danton,

Desmoulins, and the other *indulgents* went to the guillotine, Danton being saved for last. He ascended the scaffold, covered in the blood of his friends, and shouted defiantly to the crowd, "My only regret is that I am going before that rat Robespierre!" He then turned to the executioner and spoke his last words, "Don't forget to show my head to the people. It'll be well worth seeing."

Like the Roman god Saturn, the Revolution was now eating its own children, and the guillotine's appetite for heads only seemed to grow by the month.

89

The moderate *indulgent* and extremist *enragé* factions were now out of the picture, leaving Robespierre and Saint-Just with absolute, unchallenged control over the reins of government. With the no credible opposition remaining, the Reign of Terror kicked into overdrive, entering a period called the 'Great Terror.' On June 10, 1794, the Committee of Public Safety stripped away the scant legal protections afforded by the Law of Suspects with their Law of 22 Prairial. Defendants would no longer be allowed to call witnesses on their own behalf nor have attorneys present to represent them. Even worse, everything from being too lazy to being overly enthusiastic could result in a denunciation as an "enemy of the people" and indictment by the Revolutionary Tribunal. As a final capstone, the law mandated only one punishment for a guilty verdict: death. In June and July alone, the guillotine claimed over 1,500 victims as a result of the law.

Now that he was in absolute control, Robespierre took advantage of this moment to inaugurate the new State Religion of his Republic of Virtue: the Cult of the Supreme Being. Borrowing heavily from the philosophy of his heroes Rousseau and Voltaire, the Cult of the Supreme Being had no dogma but to recognize the existence of a deistic Supreme Being and the immortality of the soul. Unlike the atheistic Cult of Reason, which Robespierre despised, the Cult of the Supreme Being celebrated the civic-minded, harmonious, nature-loving society the Republic of Virtue was supposed to cultivate in its citizens. To inaugurate his new religion, Robespierre threw a suitably grand celebration.

This Festival of the Supreme Being, held on June 8, 1794, was both the height of Robespierre's vision for a utopian society and the moment his regime officially jumped the shark in the public's eye. He constructed an artificial mountain in the Champ de Mars, topped by a tree of liberty, and led the assembled congregation in a pseudo-pagan nature worshiping ceremony. Although some pointed out that this was the only time they ever saw the typically dour Robespierre happy, there were plenty of grumblings about the presumptuousness of him holding a republican high mass like a revolutionary pope. Thuriot, an old friend of Danton, summed up the popular

feeling, "It's not enough for him to be master, he has to be God."

His attempt at self-apotheosis during the Festival of the Supreme Being, combined with the rapidly escalating number of executions under the Great Terror, finally convinced Robespierre's opponents to turn against the mad philosopher-king. The French victory at the Battle of Fleurus (interesting historical aside, this was the first battle ever involving military aircraft, the French Aerostatic Corps' observation balloon *L'Entreprenant*) turned the tide of war in favor of the Republic and took away the *raison d'urgence* justifying the Terror. Unlike many other events in the French Revolution, the reason for the downfall of Robespierre was simple – people just got tired of looking over their shoulders all the time.

After hearing murmurings that there were members of the Convention seeking to dissolve the Committee of Public Safety, Robespierre gave a two-hour long rambling speech on July 26, denouncing unnamed delegates as traitors and conspirators against the Republic. Robespierre's accusations were so broad they shocked even moderate deputies. While the Incorruptible had always been susceptible to a good conspiracy theory, if he had gone completely off the deep end into the realm of paranoid delusion, all their lives were at risk. The next day Saint-Just spoke in support of Robespierre, trying to put any rumors to rest, but instead of silencing debate it provoked a revolt in the Convention hall. Robespierre attempted to speak at the rostrum, but his voice was quickly drowned out with shouts of "Down with the tyrant!" A motion for the arrest of Robespierre, Saint-Just, and their supporters went up for a voice vote and quickly passed. The virtuous dictator and his coterie ran out of the hall to avoid being mauled to death by their fellow legislators.

Robespierre, Saint-Just and their companions holed up in the Hôtel de Ville along with some loyal troops from the Paris Commune and awaited for reinforcements to arrive. Robespierre imagined that the whole of the Paris Commune and the *sans-culottes,* upon hearing of his arrest warrant, would rise up against the Convention and restore him to power. However, this mass uprising never happened. National Guardsmen loyal to the Convention surrounded the Hôtel de Ville and stormed it late that night. Much like the Nazi high command in the bunker during the fall of Berlin, the *Terroristes,* realizing their end was imminent, went about trying to kill themselves. Le Bas shot himself in the head. Augustin Robespierre (Robespierre's less famous younger brother) jumped out a window and broke both his legs. Hanriot also jumped out a window and knocked himself unconscious, landing in a pile of manure. The wheelchair-bound Couthon was found sprawled at the bottom of a flight of stairs. Even the great Robespierre attempted suicide by pistol, but the shot only managed to shatter his lower jaw. Only Saint-Just stoically awaited his arrest.

The Convention issued a decree declaring Robespierre and his allies outlaws from justice, allowing for their immediate execution without any judicial proceedings. The men were carted to the very guillotine at the Place de la Revolution where they had condemned so many others to die. Robespierre was only semi-conscious by this point, his shattered jaw held together by a soiled rag, but the crowd did not hold back. They vented their frustration and anger at the nine months of Terror by hurling insults and other more foul things at the man. Like Danton, Robespierre was forced to watch his friends die first. After he finally ascended the scaffold, the executioner tore off the bandage holding his jaw together in order to clear his neck for the blade. Several witnesses reported that Robespierre screamed in agony "like that of a dying tiger" while he was slid into place and finally silenced by the falling blade. The crowd erupted in cheers. The chief proponent of the Terror and all his cronies were now dead, hoisted by their own bloody petard.

other notable revolutionaries

JEAN-SYLVAIN BAILLY 1st Mayor of Paris. 1st to take the Tennis Court Oath.

PHILIPPE ÉGALITÉ FATHER OF FUTURE KING LOUIS PHILIPPE

JACQUES PIERRE BRISSOT GIRONDIST LEADER

CHARLOTTE CORDAY DID THE WORLD A FAVOR.

PIERRE VICTURNIEN VERGNIAUD GIRONDIST ORATOR

ANTOINE QUENTIN FOUQUIER-TINVILLE PUBLIC PROSECUTOR

MADAME ROLAND HOSTED GIRONDIST SALONS

GEORGES COUTHON RAMPED UP EXECUTIONS

JÉRÔME PÉTION de VILLENEUVE 2D MAYOR OF PARIS. EATEN BY WOLVES.

Historians call the events surrounding the downfall and execution of Robespierre the Thermidorian Reaction, named after the month of Thermidor (i.e., July) when they took place. What made Robespierre's downfall truly 'reactionary' was that it signified a definitive rejection of the radical revolutionary form of government he espoused. The Convention worked quickly to neuter and then completely abolish the Committee of Public Safety. They repealed the Law of 22nd Prairial on August 1, and suppressed the Revolutionary Tribunal. The Public Prosecutor, Fouquier-Tinville, was himself arrested, tried, and ultimately executed in spite of his Nuremburg-esque 'I was just following orders' defense. Executions for counter-revolutionary activity dropped to a trickle. As a sign of how far they had fallen, the Jacobin club was banned as disruptive to public order, and for the first time since 1793, Catholic ceremonies were celebrated in public. Everywhere the apparatus of revolutionary government collapsed and people rejoiced as some sense of normalcy returned to France.

The problem was that the country still lacked legitimate institutions. The National Convention, remember, was originally supposed to have been a temporary, constitution-drafting body. They did create the progressive Constitution of 1793, but it never actually went into effect, and now carried far too much Jacobin baggage. No, a whole new constitution would be needed yet again. Banking on the growing dissatisfaction with the course of the Revolution, royalists thought they could seize the moment and restore the Bourbon monarchy. In royalist strongholds throughout the country a 'White Terror' broke out, with Bourbon supporters meting out mob justice to their former Jacobin tormenters. However, the death of the young Dauphin, the titled but never crowned Louis XVII, put an end to their hopes of a restoration. His uncle, the Count of Provence, immediately declared himself Louis XVIII and the rightful King of France. Putting the late king's *émigré* brother on the throne – the same one who had actively conspired with Austria and Prussia to wage war against France and promised a complete restoration of the *ancien régime* once he came to power – just wasn't a realistic option. The new constitution would still be a republican one, but far more cautious and conservative than previous attempts, echoing the atmosphere of 1795.

In one of the biggest changes, for the first time France would have a bicameral legislature. Their recent experience with a runaway Convention convinced the delegates that checks and balances on a single legislative house could be a good thing. The lower house took the name 'Council of Five Hundred' and contained, you guessed it, five hundred members. The upper house gained the august title 'Council of Ancients' and contained two hundred-fifty members. The executive branch, called the 'Directory,' consisted of five directors, with one forced to retire each year by lot. On August 22, the Convention formally ratified the new Constitution of 1795.

Before it could even go into effect, the document was hugely unpopular with the public. It restricted voting to propertied males much like the Constitution of 1791, disenfranchising millions of voters. Even worse, the constitution included a measure decreeing that two-thirds of the new legislature must come from the delegates to the hated National Convention. The thought that the constitution-drafters should constitute a majority of the new legislature, before a single vote was even cast, came across as crassly political and self-serving. A constitutional crisis was brewing before the new government even formed.

In early October of 1795, a motley assortment of far-right royalist and far-left Jacobin agitators rose up in defiance of the Convention and their new constitution. By the morning of October 5, several sections of Paris had declared themselves in open insurrection, with nearly 25,000 insurgents marching on the Convention. The hastily assembled government forces only numbered 6,000, but they occupied strategic positions around the major bridges and choke points of central Paris, and they possessed something the rioters did not: artillery. Once again, at the right place at the right time, the commander of the government forces during its darkest hour was none other than the Hero of Toulon, Napoleon Bonaparte. In a desperate fight lasting over three hours, Napoleon ordered his guns to fire grapeshot (masses of small metal balls, effectively turning the cannons into oversized shotguns) directly into the onrushing crowd. While history remembers this event by Napoleon's famously aloof description of a "whiff of grapeshot," in reality the fighting was so intense he had his horse shot out from under him. When the battle was over, hundreds lay dead and Napoleon was once again hailed as the savior of the Republic. The insurrection's failure to topple the government permanently destroyed the power of the Paris Commune and *sans-culottes*.

XI

THE DIRECTORY:

A GOVERNMENT AS EXCITING

AS IT SOUNDS

On November 2, 1795, the National Convention officially dissolved itself and the new constitution went into effect, launching the period known as the Directory. The Directors' goal was to show that the Revolution had reached a culmination, and they were it. They did this by portraying themselves as the moderate, sensible choice, standing firm against both far-right royalism and far-left Jacobinism. The problem was that nobody trusted them. The two-thirds rule cast a pall of illegitimacy over the new government, causing people to believe (correctly) that the fix was in and voting was a sham. The other problem was that the country's still-unresolved financial problems had been allowed to fester under the previous revolutionary government.

Most of the nobility had emigrated, taking all their portable wealth with them and leaving their lands to lie fallow and unproductive. The anti-business policies of the Convention had also caused the wealthy bourgeoisie to take their money abroad. The economy was contracting, taxes were left uncollected, famines resulted in more food shortages, and most commodities were prioritized to the military. Even though the General Maximum was repealed in late 1794, prices continued to skyrocket due to inflation. When the Directory took office, the value of the *assignat* had fallen to 1% of par value. Government mints were churning out two billion *livres* worth of *assignats* every month, totaling a whopping thirty-four billion in circulation when the printing finally ceased in February of 1796 (there's even a tale of a printing house collapsing due to the non-stop running of the presses). The farce of the government financing its ballooning debt through printing more money, and then receiving the even more worthless paper back in taxes, had gone on for too long. The Directory tried a variety of other stopgap measures over the next two years as they attempted to transition the economy back to hard currency. Some private contractors made a killing by buying up speculative government bonds during all the fiscal chaos, making the Directory appear even less credible and competent.

Meanwhile, the population of Paris continued to starve. One working class resident wrote, "It really seems as if the time has come at last to die of hunger and cold . . . Great God, what a Republic!" Into the fray stepped the self-styled Tribune of the People, "Gracchus" Babeuf (he adopted the name from the Gracchi brothers, champions of the people during the Roman Republic). While a supporter of Robespierre and the Jacobins, Babeuf believed that they did not go far enough in ensuring economic justice for all French citizens. In many ways, Babeuf was a Communist before that term even existed. He viewed the French Revolution through the lens of class warfare and believed that it was merely the first stirrings of a much larger social revolution that would sweep the globe. The only way to achieve true equality was by abolishing private property altogether, making the State solely responsible for the ownership and distribution of goods throughout society. While it fell short of his ultimate goal of a socialist utopia, Babeuf championed implementing the Constitution of 1793 as a first step.

The out of power Jacobins and *sans-culottes* rallied to Babeuf, and by April they prepared themselves to overthrow the Directory in what they called their "Conspiracy of Equals." The elaborate coup attempt involved turning both the police force and army against the government through Babeuf's pamphleteering. The *sans-culottes* would then incite mass uprisings in the streets, with the military (or at least a substantial chunk of it) joining in, resulting in the Directory's collapse. Before it could even get off the ground, the Directors got wind of this conspiracy and for once acted decisively, quickly crushing it. Babeuf and the ringleaders were arrested, tried, and executed, but the entire episode gave the Directory a deep shock. The fact that Babeuf's conspiracy might have succeeded if given enough time showed just how deep dislike of the government ran. An air of impermanence hung about the Directory, as if

Gracchus Babeuf

everybody knew it was just a temporary placeholder for something else. As to what that something else might be, extremists of all stripes filled the void, attempting to win the public to their cause. It was under this cloud that the first elections took place in the spring of 1797.

It was now painfully obvious that the unpopular Directory was wholly reliant on the army and its generals. Far from the rag-tag force that lost nearly every battle it fought in 1792, the French Army of 1797 was composed of crack veteran troops and some very able commanders. In a parallel to modern Turkey or Egypt, the army envisioned itself as the guarantor of the Republic against both far-left and far-right extremists. The army assumed an ever more prominent role in society as they put down internal rebellions, beat back enemy threats, and increasingly funded government coffers through plundering their foreign conquests. Since 1796, Napoleon had been barnstorming through northern Italy as he knocked the Kingdom of Sardinia-Piedmont out of the war and was taking the fight directly to Austria. He was a rising star in the army and everybody (particularly Napoleon himself) realized how the reliant the Directory had become on his support and continued victories.

The election of 1797 was a disastrous defeat for incumbents. Of the 150 or so grandfathered delegates from the National Convention, only eleven won re-election. Nearly half of the new legislature consisted of people with no prior experience in public office, reflecting a deep distrust of the political class. Catching nearly everyone by surprise was the royalist resurgence. Left for dead after nearly five years in the wilderness, conservative delegates supporting some sort of restoration of the monarchy won nearly two hundred seats. While divided in their ultimate aims, the royalists were united in their peace platform. The country had been at war with her neighbors for far too long, depriving her of not only blood and treasure, but stability as well. If peace required France to barter away some of her military conquests to attain it, they were all for it. This stance, of course, did nothing to endear the royalists to the army and its ever more influential generals.

Napoleon, applying his military genius to the political arena, formed an alliance with three of the Directors, Barras, Reubell, and La Révellière, to "save the Republic from Royalism." Supported by Napoleon's troops, the Directors denounced several royalist leaders as traitors to the Revolution, had them arrested, and permanently relocated them to French Guiana. They annulled the results of the election of 1797 as a matter of "national emergency" and appointed left-wing deputies to fill the vacant seats. While nearly bloodless, this 'Coup of 18 Fructidor' effectively destroyed any veneer of legitimacy the new government had. The illusion of democratic government, always tenuous at best, was now gone completely. The interests of the army and the Directors were clearly one and inseparable. The Directors used the army to maintain themselves in power, and the army expected the Directors to pursue policies favorable towards it. Historians call this post-coup government the 'Second Directory' since it kept all the legal formalisms provided in the Constitution of 1795, but functioned outside the boundaries of the law.

The Second Directory's most astonishing feat was their proficiency in making a populace that already hated them hate them even more. On September 30, 1797, the Directory took the drastic, although necessary, step that Louis XVI convened the Estates-General in an attempt to avoid; they finally declared bankruptcy. While they tried to dress it up to make it look better than it was (not a full bankruptcy, but only a 'reorganization' where they'd pay off two-thirds of the debt in worthless *assignats*) everyone saw through it. Whereas all prior governments had attempted to preserve the debt, Mirabeau's famed "national treasure," at all costs, the Directory's bankruptcy shattered public confidence. However, it did finally allow the State to get its fiscal house in order for the first time in several decades, balancing the books and putting an end to the era of rampant hyperinflation.

The alliance between the army and civilian government also meant that the Second Directory was a time of increasing militarism. Belgium, the Netherlands, the left bank of the Rhine, Switzerland, and northern Italy were all either turned into French client states or annexed outright. Even Rome proved too tempting a target, falling in short order with the recalcitrant Pope Pius VI taken prisoner (he would later die in captivity). Loot from foreign adventures flowed into the capital; the cycle of war, conquest, pillage, and tribute quickly became self-perpetuating as the Directory factored plunder into the yearly budgets. Napoleon's stunning victories at the battles of Arcole and Rivoli forced Austria to cede most of her Italian possessions to France in the Treaty of Campo Formio. The fact that Napoleon agreed to allow monarchial Austria to absorb the ancient Republic of Venice as part of their agreement perfectly demonstrates his penchant for pragmatism over ideology. All too eager to get this ambitious young general as far away from them as possible, the Directors agreed to Napoleon's plan to seize Egypt and thus drive a wedge between England and her colonial possessions in India. Meanwhile, at home the Directory grew ever more dictatorial, closely monitoring the results of elections and freely annulling them if they viewed the winning candidate as too extreme either right or left.

By 1799, the Directory's belligerence and military aggression was coming back to bite them. Russia had finally joined the coalition against France and convinced Austria to join them in declaring war, repudiating the Treaty of Campo Formio before the ink even had a chance to dry. While Napoleon defeated the Egyptian forces at the Battle of the Pyramids and occupied Cairo, British Admiral Horatio Nelson smashed his fleet in the Nile, stranding Napoleon with his army far from home. News was even bad from across the Atlantic, after a string of diplomatic insults and naval skirmishes between France and the United States threatened to escalate into full-scale war. In response to this crisis, the Directory began passing emergency measures that looked suspiciously similar to those during the Reign of Terror. Press censorship, anti-religious prosecution, forced military conscription: all returned to much public scorn. The Directory even passed a Law of Hostages, which was in effect a new Law of Suspects just with a different name. With no other options left, the Directors took the step they most feared to save their own skins – they recalled Napoleon Bonaparte from Egypt to ride in on his white horse as Savior of the Republic once again. Anticipating this, he was already on a ship back to France before the letter even arrived.

Napoleon knew better than to let a good crisis go to waste.

After years of absence from the scene, the Abbé Sieyès re-emerged. The wily priest had done an admirable job of keeping his head on his shoulders during the Reign of Terror, going so far as to renounce Catholicism during the height of dechristian-ization (his quote, "I survived"). However, Sieyès was no radical, but rather a strong supporter of the conservative, bourgeois Con-stitution of 1791. The events of 1799 made him fear that the Re-public was backsliding towards Jacobinism and required a strong hand to guide the Revolution to a successful conclusion. He imagined Napoleon to be a fellow pragmatist and useful tool to ac-complish his goal. It just so hap-pened that Napoleon thought ex-actly the same thing about Sieyès.

Napoleon returned to Paris as a conquering hero, the Republic's one undefeated general who had triumphantly returned to save it from rapine and ruin. Sieyès, recently elected to a Directorial position (highly ironic considering that he was a habitual basher of the Directory) quickly approached him with his plan for a coup. Also in on the conspiracy was another member of the Class of 1789, the former-Bishop Talleyrand, and Napoleon's brother, Lucien Bonaparte, then President of the Council of Five Hundred. Their plan was this: Sieyès would present 'evidence' of a far-reaching Jacobin plot to infiltrate the Directory and overthrow the government. He would then declare that the legislature must select an entirely new panel of Directors to ensure none of them had been compromised, and immediately resign his own position as a show of good faith. After some pressure, the other four Directors agreed to do so as well. Lucien Bonaparte would propose that the legislature move to the Château of Saint-Cloud outside Paris for their deliberations, ostensibly to guard against possible uprisings, while Napoleon and his troops accompanied, providing escort and protection. Thus, the wheels were set in motion for the Coup of 18 of Brumaire (November 9), which would usher in the downfall of the Republic and the rise of Napoleon.

The first part of their plan went off without a hitch, but the next day it nearly all fell apart. On November 10, the plan was for Napoleon to enter the legislature and propose they establish an emergency government with himself and Sieyès as its heads. Figuring that it would be best to start with the more conservative – and presumably more supportive – Council of Ancients, Napoleon presented his proposal to them. The delegates looked on in silence while he talked, and when the general finished his rather wooden speech, they heckled him.

For all Napoleon's strengths, he was never very good at taking criticism. As the typically calculating general became more and more agitated, he got sloppy. He was used to giving orders, not being questioned, so he abruptly declared that the debate was over and told the Ancients to appoint him provisional head of government. When one of them shouted "But what about the Constitution?" Napoleon sarcastically snapped back that it was already dead, and they were the ones who had killed it.

Not getting the reception he had expected from the Ancients, Napoleon marched into the Council of Five Hundred, hoping to win them over with the support of his brother. He could not have been more wrong. As soon as he started speaking, cries of "Traitor!" and "Outlaw him!" erupted from the far more radical lower chamber. When he refused to cede the rostrum, a number of deputies physically assaulted Napoleon, forcing his troops to drag him from the fray. Emerging from the chamber with torn clothing and a dramatic trickle of blood running from his lip, Lucien Bonaparte declared to the troops that the Council was in revolt and had tried to assassinate their beloved commander. With all pretense gone, the soldiers stormed the chamber and forcibly dispersed the legislature. Several hours later, they reassembled a small quorum of loyal members to vote in favor of a commission to write a new constitution, vesting governing power in Napoleon, Sieyès, and Ducos as the three Consuls (if not exactly amigos). While it wasn't pretty, the coup had worked and the Directory was no more.

XII

NAPOLEON'S RISE:

THE FRENCH CONSULATE

While the French Republic would technically survive until 1804, from this point on it was a RINO: Republican in Name Only. Perhaps the greatest confirmation of this fact was the complete lack of popular anger over the coup. The Parisian population, previously so quick to rise up against tyranny (both real and imagined), did absolutely nothing when a general forcibly overthrew the government and put himself in charge. The revolutionary energy simmering in 1789, percolating in 1791, and finally boiling over in 1793-94, had all but fizzled out by the turn of the century. The truth was that after a decade of foreign war, civil war, economic crisis, famine, and political persecution, the people were sick of revolution and wanted to get back to their normal lives. Napoleon recognized this and promised a competent government that would ensure order and stability. All he asked for in exchange was absolute power.

The first thing Napoleon needed to do was outmaneuver Sieyès in forming the new constitution so that he came out on top. Sieyès was a moderate conservative at heart and made no bones about the fact that he favored a constitutional monarchy on the 1791 model. Only such a system could provide

the stability necessary for his ideal society "devoted to the pursuit of material comfort." Sieyès' proposal was for the creation of a 'Grand Elector' as Head of State, who would serve for life and act as a kind of republican king. Other than ceremonial functions, the Grand Elector's only real duty was the appointment of state officers, including the two Consuls who would share executive power, one dealing with domestic and the other with foreign affairs. Napoleon had no intention of serving at the pleasure of anyone else; instead, he proposed a system of three Consuls, one of whom would sit above the rest as First Consul (guess who that would be?). Napoleon won support for his system, which became the final version.

It only took the commission assigned to draft the new constitution a month to complete it. Rather than have a legislative body vote on its approval, as had been done in the past, Napoleon instead pushed for approval of the constitution via nationwide plebiscite. This established a precedent that Napoleon would utilize his entire career and later became an essential feature of Bonapartism – the use of plebiscites to legitimize expansions of power. By appealing directly to the people, Napoleon could circumvent rival politicians (whom he had little patience for anyway) while simultaneously portraying himself as a populist. The whole exercise was a charade since the constitution (known as the Constitution of 1799 or the Year VIII) went into effect 'provisionally' prior to approval anyway, and the vote in January of 1800 returned the highly dubious result of 99.9% in favor of adoption.

In formulating this new government with himself at the head, we see Napoleon's long-term strategy playing out. Unlike Julius Caesar and Alexander the Great, two other great generals who rose to political prominence, Napoleon did not have the advantage of being born into a rich and powerful family. Hailing from the lower Italian nobility, he would likely have been stuck in a midlevel officer position his entire career if not for the Revolution. Unlike most of his fellow officers who chose to emigrate, Napoleon seized the opportunity it presented. By doing so he formed an entirely new breed, the self-made leader, and made up the rules as he went along. Napoleon prided himself from a young age on having an intuitive understanding of human nature, and he used it to his advantage. He knew most people could care less about Jacobinism, or royalism, or any other 'ism' for that matter. What they cared about was having enough to eat, a steady job, a roof over their heads, safety for them and their families, and freedom to practice their religion. If he could just ensure those needs were met, the vast majority of the population would support him, regardless of ideology. He also knew that while most people liked some aspects of the Revolution – the abolition of feudalism and guarantee of basic rights for instance – they longed for the grandeur, prestige, and stability the monarchy offered. It was this ability to reconcile tradition with progress while playing both extremes against the middle that made Napoleon such a formidable political force.

The new French Consulate self-consciously modeled itself on ancient Rome. Napoleon admired the Romans and saw post-Revolutionary France as carrying on their legacy. The government itself took its name from the Consuls, the two-person executive of the Roman Republic. In addition to the Consuls, there was also a Senate in the Roman tradition, which Sieyès would head up as a consolation prize. However, all real governing power belonged to Napoleon as First Consul. From this point until 1815, the saga of France's continuing revolutions is so closely interwoven with the story of Napoleon that it is nearly impossible to pull them apart.

Much like the Directory had (unsuccessfully) attempted before him, Napoleon wished to portray his reign as the Revolution's successful conclusion. To add credibility to this argument, he needed to end the two things tearing France apart since 1792 – religious strife and foreign war. In the same way as Robespierre, Napoleon was not a religious man, but he understood how important the rituals of Catholicism were to most French people. If anything was responsible for the epidemic of popular revolts against the government in the countryside, it was the policy of dechristianization. It was wholly unenforceable outside the large cities, and it gave the priests and royalists an easy way to caricature the Republic as being an agent of Satan. If Napoleon could restore relations between France and the Roman Catholic Church, it would both boost the legitimacy of the Republic itself and shore up his own reputation as a diplomat and statesman. An expert reader of people, he knew that the new Pope, Pius VII, was eager to make a deal.

The Church at the turn of the 19th century was facing its most serious crisis since the Protestant Reformation. Godless revolutionaries occupied Rome and the last Pope, Pius VI, had actually died while in French captivity. Of the traditional Catholic powers, Spain was in terminal decline, Austria looked weaker than ever, and France was now her greatest enemy. Napoleon knew that if he made Pius VII an offer of reconciliation, the Pontiff would have to take it. Negotiations between the Pope and First Consul began in November of 1800, and dragged on for nine months as both sides postured, gave ultimatums, stormed out of the room, and angrily returned to the bargaining table. Yet on July 15, both Napoleon and Pius VII signed the Concordat of 1801, restoring full relations between France and the Holy See. As part of the agreement, Napoleon recognized Catholicism as the religion of the "great majority of the French" (although he refused to make it the official state religion like the Pope wanted), agreed to abolish the Revolutionary Calendar (which nobody really liked anyway), and restored the Pope's ability to appoint bishops (of limited use since the State still nominated them). The Pope agreed to recognize the Consulate as the sole legitimate government of France, give up the Church's claims on confiscated lands, and have priests swear a loyalty oath to the State in exchange for their salaries. Like all good agreements, nobody was entirely happy with the results, but it rallied popular support behind Napoleon's regime while allowing him to undermine both the royalist and Jacobin opposition by taking the religious issue off the table.

With peace at home, Napoleon set himself to the task of making peace abroad. France had been constantly at war since 1792. The only way to break the cycle of extremism and create the kind of stability needed to consolidate the gains of the Revolution was to end the uncertainty of war. None of the Coalition members felt much inclined to make peace with Republican France, so Napoleon had to impose it on them. Following another lighting campaign through northern Italy, Napoleon's army crushed the Austrians at the closely fought Battle of Marengo. In addition to driving Austria out of Italy, Napoleon milked the battle for every ounce of propaganda value it was worth. Marengo solidified Napoleon's hold on power, causing both his political enemies and rival generals to fall in line. Austria sued for peace once again, ceding even more of her German and Italian territories to France.

With Russia quietly bowing out of the war a year prior, Great Britain remained the only belligerent power left. The British people were sick of war and her merchants wanted the resumption of normal trade. Napoleon capitalized on this desire, sending peace feelers out through French foreign minister Talleyrand. Parliament decided to accept, sending Lord Cornwallis to negotiate on behalf of His Majesty's Government (yes, the same Cornwallis who surrendered to George Washington at Yorktown). Napoleon sent his older brother Joseph to represent the French Republic. The budget deadline was fast approaching and Parliament needed to know whether to appropriate war funds for the next fiscal year. Joseph used this to his advantage and purposefully dragged out negotiations, hoping that by running down the clock he could force Cornwallis to accept an unfavorable peace treaty, which is exactly what happened. Both countries signed the Treaty of Amiens on March 25, 1802, inaugurating a single year of uneasy peace between England and France. It would be the only time the two countries were not at war between 1793 and 1815.

Although Napoleon successfully ended the wars abroad (for a time) and restored peace at home, he still faced constant threats to his rule. In the span of two months, the First Consul faced two serious assassination attempts – a stabbing and a bombing, the latter of which resulted in the deaths of several innocent bystanders. While Napoleon's military victories and the restoration of order at home made him extremely popular with the French people, he needed a way to solidify his hold on government.

Using the assassination attempts to show that there were extremists seeking to overthrow the government, Napoleon pushed for an amendment to the Constitution, changing his position from First Consul to Consul for Life. The proposal was once again put to a national referendum where it passed with over 99% approval. On August 2, 1802, the Constitution of the Year X went into effect, abolishing all pretext of republican government. The monarchy was now restored in all but name. The only thing left for Napoleon to do was put a crown on his head, which he did two years later.

XIII

NAPOLEON'S TRIUMPH:

THE FIRST FRENCH EMPIRE

I n 1803, the tenuous peace between England and France finally broke down. Neither side signed the Treaty of Amiens in good faith and both sought to circumvent its terms whenever possible; never a recipe for success. England irked Napoleon by refusing to remove her troops from Malta and Egypt as agreed. The British, for their part, complained that Napoleon's invasion of Haiti, sale of France's Louisiana territory to the United States, and continued interventions in both Switzerland and Italy were needlessly belligerent. In May, Britain sent Napoleon an ultimatum to stop at once. When he refused as expected, Britain declared war.

For a good long while, the war was fairly boring. Napoleon assembled an army at Boulogne on the Channel coast and trained them for the anticipated invasion of England. As the troops waited, he continued to build up his fleet and even seriously considered an aerial assault of the island via hot air balloon. The British relied on their well-worn anti-Napoleonic strategy – maintain mastery of the seas and use their huge wallet to bankroll France's enemies. In the meantime, another momentous event happened on the home front that would permanently alter the course of the Revolution. The First French Republic was about to transform into the First French Empire.

In 1804, French police uncovered an elaborate international plot to overthrow Napoleon's government and put the Duke d'Enghien, a minor Bourbon price, on the throne. Financed by the British once again, what made the plot so terrifying to Napoleon was that two of his generals, Moreau and Pichegru, were in on the conspiracy. While there was little evidence connecting the Duke directly to the plot, Napoleon could take no chances. Even though he was residing in a tiny principality on the German side of the Rhine, Napoleon had the Duke arrested, tried, and executed along with the rest of the conspirators. This caused an international uproar and indirectly served Britain's war aims by driving previously neutral powers away from the French. Paradoxically, it also gave Napoleon the justification he needed to make his office hereditary.

SURELY YOU WOULDN'T SHOOT A PUPPY!

Duc D'Enghien

The "Duc d'Enghien affair" was the third serious attempt to kill or overthrow Napoleon in as many years. While he was wildly popular personally, Napoleon feared that the entire edifice he had created would come crashing down upon his death. The royalists and Jacobins would surely rush in to fill the power vacuum left by his demise, plunging France into chaos once again. The only solution that would ensure a stable future for France and safeguard the values of the Revolution was the most ironic one imaginable – La République must have a Monarch.

While seemingly strange, the creation of the Empire was the height of Napoleonic pragmatism – win the broad middle, ignore and marginalize both the far-left and the far-right. Remember, the majority of the bourgeois delegates to the National Assembly back in 1789 were champions of a constitutional monarchy. Napoleon knew he could win over liberal royalists by restoring the prestige of the throne while simultaneously maintaining the loyalty of moderate republicans with his vow to uphold the values of the Revolution. He also never shared the Jacobin fantasy that a pan-republican Europe was standing by, just waiting for France to liberate her. In order for France's post-revolutionary future to be secure, it needed to normalize relations with its neighbors, nearly all of which were monarchies. Napoleon hoped that by becoming Emperor he could legitimize his rule amongst Europe's crowned heads and end their reflexive suspicion of all things revolutionary. Finally, we can't remove Napoleon's massive ego from the calculation. He believed (or at least led everyone else to believe) that he was a Man of Destiny, fated to do great things. 'Emperor' is a far more impressive title than 'Life Consul,' and one which carries infinitely more majesty, mystique, and gravitas. What better way could Napoleon humble the blue-blooded monarchs of Europe, who commonly addressed him by the derisive name "Corsican Usurper," than to crown himself in glory over the greatest empire Europe had known since the time of Charlemagne?

To maintain credibility, Napoleon had to give this shiny new title a suitably republican gloss. He did not simply announce the change, but instead put it to a plebiscite and had the people decide. The measure passed with over 99% approval yet again (surprise, surprise) and the Senate issued its proclamation of the Empire on May 18, 1804. Since the French were so fond of new constitutions, the Imperial Constitution of the XII replaced the Life Consular Constitution of the Year X, which itself had replaced the First Consular Constitution of the Year VIII. To indicate that his power derived from the People rather than by Divine Right, he opted for the more egalitarian-sounding title 'Emperor of the French' rather than 'Emperor of France.' Still, such a title required a certain degree of pomp to inaugurate, so Napoleon planned an elaborate coronation ceremony to take place in France's grandest cathedral, the Notre Dame de Paris.

Rather than hearken back to the Bourbon dynasty, Napoleon choose a unique blend of imperial Roman and medieval Carolingian pageantry to link up France's glorious past with its bright new future. To lend a religious air to the coronation, he invited Pope Pius VII to attend, but only his presence was necessary. If there is one aspect of Napoleon's coronation that history remembers best, it would be him placing the crown upon his own head

to signify the independence of his rule. To top it all off, he took a loyalty oath to the Constitution and the Republic, administered by the President of the Senate, thus becoming the first person since the Caesars to be both an emperor and a republican at the same time. The following year he would also be crowned King of Italy at the Duomo in Milan, further solidifying his control over the whole of his multi-national 'Grand Empire.'

Meanwhile, France faced a whole sea of troubles abroad as British money drew Austria and Russia back into the fray. Their entry into the war (along with England's adamant refusal to vacate the Channel) forced Napoleon to abandon his lofty plans for an invasion of the British Isles, turning his 300,000-man army west. In the course of only three months, he won a series of battles against the Austrians, managing to encircle and capture their entire army at Ulm. Never one to rest on his laurels, Napoleon struck towards Vienna, hoping to goad the remaining Austrian and Russian forces into a defense of the capital. They took the bait and were utterly crushed at the Battle of Austerlitz, widely considered Napoleon's greatest victory and most superb tactical masterpiece. Austria and Russia quickly made peace, with Austria forced to give up a huge chunk of property in exchange yet again. Little did Napoleon know that just two weeks before his victory at Austerlitz, France lost nearly her entire fleet at the Battle of Trafalgar, ending any hopes of ever invading England.

Prussia had been fighting with Austria for control of the various German states ('Germany' was not yet a single country) for the previous several decades and wasn't about to allow the French to dominate German affairs. They rashly declared war in 1806, and immediately came to regret it.

The Prussian army, once the mightiest in Europe under Frederick the Great fifty years prior, was completely destroyed by Napoleon at the battle of Jena-Auerstadt. In his shortest campaign yet, it took Napoleon less than twenty days to capture Berlin and knock Prussia out of the war. With Russia left as the only power opposing France, the Tsar came to the table in 1807, signing the Treaty of Tilsit and leaving Napoleon as the undisputed master of the continent.

After all the fighting, the parties took a two-year breather. Finally in 1809, British cash enticed Austria into yet another disastrous war against France. Napoleon once again crushed their armies and Austria sued for peace, purchasing it with more land and money. However, this time Napoleon wanted something more. He was sick of fighting them and wanted real assurance that the Austrian Emperor, Francis I, wouldn't just stab him in the back again like he had done previously – on three separate occasions. He pressed for a full alliance between the French and Austrian Empires, and to ensure Francis' good faith, this prodigy of the Revolution used a trick right out of the old regime playbook. He would marry the Emperor's eldest daughter, Marie Louise, to join the two dynasties together. Yes, the Corsican upstart who had defeated this once-mighty power on four separate occasions would now become the Emperor of Austria's son-in-law. He divorced his wife Josephine, whom he had soured on after she repeatedly failed to get pregnant, and married the 19-year-old princess on April 1, 1810. It's hard not to see the irony going from King Louis XVI and his Austrian wife, Marie Antoinette, to Emperor Napoleon I and his Austrian wife, Marie Louise. While the marriage was a political one, she did bear him a son within the first year and their marriage brought a period of peace and stability to the continent, leaving England as the only impediment to French hegemony over Europe. The French Empire had reached the height of its dominance and glory.

Two years of peace will follow (1810-1812), so this is a good time for us to pause from our discussion of military affairs and talk about Napoleon's domestic reforms – which ultimately had a far more lasting impact than his famous victories. Even before Brumaire, Napoleon had shown a keen eye for civilian government. In this way, he was very different from his hero, Alexander the Great, who was a conqueror first and a statesman second. Napoleon actually enjoyed governing and had a very specific vision of what he wanted his empire to be.

His most far-reaching domestic reform was the creation of the French Civil Code, known to posterity as the *Code Napoléon*. Years after his glory days, while living in exile on the island of St. Helena, the deposed Emperor wistfully recalled, "Waterloo will wipe out the memory of my forty victories, but that which nothing can wipe out is my Civil Code." In order to be a truly great leader and not just a great general, Napoleon wished to be a lawgiver in the tradition of Hammurabi and Justinian. He personally sat through meetings of the drafting commission and guided development of the code throughout. After its final approval and promulgation in 1804, Napoleon was so proud of the finished product that he directed every citizen of the Empire should receive a copy. It is not hard to see why the Emperor was such a fan, as it quite literally codified his own predilections in the rule of law. The old legal pastiche of regional customs and royal diktats were gone, replaced by easy-to-understand rules of universal application. Napoleonic pragmatism was front and center as he appeased both conservatives (severely curtailing the rights of women and restricting divorce) and liberals (protecting rights to property, speech, and due process of the law). The vein running through the entire code was the centrality of the State to public life – a very Napoleonic sentiment. No longer did laws come from priests, kings, or (worst of all) self-interested politicians, but rather from the State itself, enforced by an ever-expanding Imperial Bureaucracy, in accordance with Napoleon's preference for administration over politics. While subject to substantial revisions, the influence of the *Code Napoléon* was so far reaching that it still forms the legal foundation of most non-Anglophone countries today.

While His Majesty the Emperor Napoleon I had certainly evolved a lot from the firebrand, republican general of 1793, his Jacobin tendencies still surfaced from time to time, no matter how hard he tried to bury them. One area where this was most true was in public education. Prior to the French Revolution, Europe had a number of universities with pedigrees extending back to the Middle Ages, but nearly all of them were controlled by the Church. The University of Paris was one of the largest and most prestigious, but also had a history of poor town-gown relations – one of the most famous incidents occurring in 1229, after a group of drunken college students got into a fight with a tavern owner over an unpaid bar tab during Mardi Gras, which quickly escalated into an alcohol-fueled riot. During the height of dechristianization in 1794, the National Convention abolished all Church-operated schools and placed education under the purview of the State. They even created the three tiered system of primary, secondary, and tertiary education we still use today: "There shall be established in the Republic three progressive degrees of instruction; the first for the knowledge indispensable to artisans and workmen of all kinds; the second for further knowledge necessary to those intending to embrace the other professions of society; and the third for those branches of instruction the study of which is not within the reach of all men." The Convention also created three of France's now famous *Grands Écoles,* or "Great Schools" of higher education: the *École Normale Supérieure* (for education), the *École Polytechnique* (for engineering), and the *Conservatoire National des Arts et Métiers* (for science and industry).

Napoleon shared the Convention's belief that a good citizen was an educated citizen and desired, in typical Napoleonic fashion, to centralize France's disparate institutions into a single educational system. He established a system of high schools known as *lycées,* which would teach a standardized curriculum of Greek, Latin, History, Rhetoric, Logic, Math, and the Physical Sciences across the Empire. At the end of their time at the *lycée,* students were expected to pass a rigorous exam in order to receive their baccalauréat (still the bane of every French student today rigorously studying for *'le bac'*). After receiving their *baccalauréat,* students could then pursue higher education at one of the *grands écoles* or a secularized university, known as an academy (the Sorbonne dates from this time). In 1808, the regime officially consolidated all of the *lycées,* academies, and *grands écoles* into a single Imperial University of France (think of it as a forerunner of the Department of Education). While theoretically open to all people regardless of rank or class, in actuality only well-off families could afford the expense of higher education. The cost of tuition priced out all poor and most middle class students, while the limited scholarships issued by the State primarily went to sons of the civil or military elite. Still, it was a huge improvement over the old regime educational model of non-nobles need not apply.

If Napoleon's attitude towards public education was the Emperor at his most progressive, then his creation of a new nobility was him at his most reactionary. While Napoleon's most staunchly republican supporters might have shifted uncomfortably at his imperial coronation or grumbled over his re-establishment of Catholicism in France, they howled when he brought back titles of nobility. After all, one of the Revolution's earliest and proudest accomplishments was the abolition of feudal distinctions between citizens, now enshrined in the principle of *Egalité*. Wasn't restoring the nobility a betrayal of everything they had fought and bled for over the past two decades?

Never one to let opposition stifle his carefully laid plans, the idea of creating an imperial nobility of his own proved too tempting for a glory hound like Napoleon to resist. Napoleon's real 'complex' was that his brother monarchs never accepted the legitimacy of his reign. In their view, he was a rowdy, uninvited guest crashing their royal cocktail party, and they would do everything possible to see him ejected from it. Napoleon was acutely aware of this and tried to overcompensate with the most pompous and elaborate court ceremonial on the Continent. Perhaps by creating a new nobility (with suitably grand titles of his own design) he could woo monarchial Europe to his side and further cement Imperial France's role as its leading power.

The ability to award titles of nobility also gave the Emperor a cheap new form of social control. He knew that the Revolution had not quenched the burning desire of ambitious men to set themselves above and apart from all others. What sweeter way to satisfy this craving than by dangling the forbidden fruit of a principality or duchy in front of them? In this way, he could keep his supporters loyal and pacify his critics by tying their own self-interest to the continued survival of his regime.

Restoring the nobility was a hard sell, even for Napoleon, so he brought it back gradually. First, he created an institution that has survived to the present day as the highest award France can bestow: *La Légion d'honneur* (the Legion of Honor). In a way that is classically Napoleon, he fused together the medieval chivalric orders with a Roman organization into a modern system of awards based on merit and service to the State. Disparaged by its critics as being a "mere bauble," Napoleon famously replied that, "It is with such baubles that men are led."

The next step was the creation of 'senatoriates,' landed estates awarded to especially influential senators in recognition of their high position. After this he became more brazen and started adding various titles – princes beginning in 1804 (mostly for members of the newly minted House of Bonaparte and Marshals of the Empire), dukes in 1806, and finally counts, barons, and knights in 1808. However, unlike the old nobility of past glories, this was a nobility open to all who accomplished great deeds. In this way, Napoleon could create an aristocracy based on service to the State (and vicariously to himself as Head of State) and owing its status to the Emperor's good graces. It also helped destroy the power of the old regime nobility by declaring their order obsolete and replacing it with a new one.

To finance all these grand projects (and maintain public order) Napoleon needed to strengthen France's ever-precarious economy. While no economic expert, Napoleon's instinctive grasp of human psychology led him to understand the importance confidence plays in stimulating growth. When the economy is stable, investors with excess capital will feel confident channeling their money into (hopefully) productive enterprises, and consumers will be confident enough in their own financial circumstances to spend extra money on goods and services. A stable economy required a stable currency, and the best guarantor of stable currency is to link its value to a commodity with a (relatively) stable price – i.e., precious metal. In 1803, the newly formed Bank of France issued coinage, pegging its value to that of gold and silver. Known as the 'Germinal Franc,' the coin proved so popular that it survived Napoleon by more than a century.

One of the most persistent criticisms of Napoleon's rule is that he focused too much on military matters while shunning the financial and industrial innovations breaking out in England and the United States. In reality, this was only partially true. While Napoleon's primary focus was agriculture rather than industry (not surprising since agriculture constituted over 90% of France's GDP at the time), and he tended to be extremely conservative when it came to trade, deficit financing and paper money, he did implement a number of measures to modernize the economy. The Bank of France, established in 1800, was the country's first real central bank with a monopoly on issuing currency. Equally important was the creation of the 'Sinking Fund,' which purchased government bonds in order to maintain a steady interest rate, similar to what the Federal Reserve does today. These institutions encouraged private borrowing and put some predictability into government financing. Napoleon also never shied away from offering generous subsidies to favored industries and implementing high tariffs to protect them from foreign competition, in many ways the forerunner of the 20th-century *dirigisme* policies of Charles de Gaulle. While French businessmen sometimes chafed at the State's excessive interventionism in the economy, it was the first place they ran to for help against cheaper British imports. Even though French industrial production in 1810 had nearly doubled since 1789, business' attitude towards the State remained largely unchanged from the days of Louis XVI when a textile manufacturer shouted to the King, "Sire, leave us alone, but protect us a lot!"

Napoleon was certainly a ruler who believed in protecting a lot. England had long been France's greatest economic rival, so to turn the tables on the British (a country he contemptuously referred to as a "nation of shopkeepers"), Napoleon issued a directive known as the Milan Decree in 1807, ordering all European ports closed to trade with the United Kingdom. This 'Continental System' had the dual goal of depriving England of her trading wealth while establishing a common marketplace where goods could flow freely across borders – a precursor to the European Union. The problem was that the system was not mutually beneficial in conception, or even truly economic at its core, but rather a war measure meant to enrich France and starve England at the expense of every other country in Europe. As you can likely imagine, France's shotgun allies in Prussia, Austria, and Russia chafed at the requirement that they purchase more expensive French goods over cheaper British imports. The British struck back by blockading French ports, even violating the laws of the sea by stopping neutral vessels engaged in trade with France (eventually leading to war with the United States in 1812).

The year 1812 for the French Empire was truly Dickensian in being both the best and worst of times. Marie-Louise did what Josephine could not do and gave birth to a son the year prior, quickly given the title King of Rome and Heir to the Empire. With his line of succession now secure, the once restless Napoleon grew more complacent. The Emperor's thinning hair and expanding waistline seemed physical manifestations of his Empire's own growing decadence. While on the cultural and economic fronts, France was the strongest it had been since the Revolution began, cracks were starting to show in her foreign policy. Portugal had refused to take part in the Continental System and invited the British in to help them resist. This exacerbated the already serious 'Spanish ulcer' of civil war on the Iberian Peninsula, as Catholic and royalist partisans engaged in a bloody civil war against the French occupation. Regardless of how many troops Napoleon threw into the mess, Spain was a black hole that continued to suck up men and resources. The brilliant British commander Arthur Wellesley drove the French from Madrid in 1812, after smashing King Joseph Bonaparte's army at the Battle of Salamanca, winning for himself the title Duke of Wellington. With the Spanish capital lost and their armies losing battle after battle to Wellington, the French could no longer maintain the pretext of control over their rebellious satellite kingdom; the entire Grand Empire suddenly looked very vulnerable.

Tsar ALexander I

Europe's Heart-Throb

Tsar Alexander I had signed the Treaty of Tilsit with Napoleon in 1807 at sufferance and had quietly been waiting for his time to pounce like a caged Siberian tiger. Napoleon's creation of a semi-independent Polish state, the Grand Duchy of Warsaw, was a stick in the eye to the Tsar who saw Poland as part of Russia's sphere of influence. Inspired by the Spanish/Portuguese example, Russia threw down the gauntlet in 1812, repudiating the Continental System and opening up their ports to British trade. Napoleon reacted exactly how the Tsar expected him to react; he declared war and prepared an invasion force to defeat his last remaining rival on the continent. Unlike the five previous coalitions against Napoleon, all parties knew that this time something was different. There would be no gentlemanly treaty signed at a stately palace after a battle or two. The endgame had arrived and there could be only two possible outcomes: the Emperor Napoleon would be prevail and reign as the undisputed Master of Europe, or the Coalition would send the Corsican Usurper packing once and for all. More men would fight and die in this War of the Sixth Coalition than in any previous conflict.

The force Napoleon raised for the invasion of Russia was the largest ever assembled up to that point, numbering over 600,000 men. This *Grande Armeé* was truly pan-European, reflecting the multiethnic composition of the French Empire and her satellites. Over half of the troops to accompany the Emperor in his campaign were of Italian, German, Polish, Dutch, and Spanish origin. Facing him were about 200,000 troops of the Russian Imperial Army. Although outnumbered 3 to 1, Alexander refused to give

Napoleon the chance to smash his army in one big battle, instead trading territory for time as he gave ground in a fighting retreat, slowly drawing the invading forces deeper and deeper into the vast Russian interior.

The invasion commenced on June 24, 1812, and from the start, the poor condition of the roads took a toll on the troops. The native Cossack cavalry from the Russian steppes raided the supply lines and slowed the French advance. After a number of inconclusive but bloody battles, French forces captured the city of Vilnius on June 28. His peace offers to the Tsar completely ignored, Napoleon pressed onwards, subjecting his men to alternating periods of brutal summer heat waves punctuated by torrential downpours that turned the ground into muddy soup. Making matters worse, the retreating Russian generals employed scorched earth tactics, burning the land in their wake and leaving nothing for the French to forage amidst the destruction. When Napoleon arrived at Smolensk on August 18, his army had already lost over 150,000 men.

Conventional military wisdom dictated that he fortify Smolensk, summon up reinforcements to replace his losses, and hunker down for the winter. However, by 1812, even the seemingly inexhaustible resources of the French Empire had been driven to the breaking point. He could expect relatively few reinforcements to arrive, while Russian forces could easily replace their own losses. Furthermore, he was already having a difficult time keeping his army fed. Without the ability to forage, his men would surely starve over the long winter. With his empire at stake, Napoleon the gambler came back. He rejected the conventional wisdom and ordered an advance deeper into the Russian wilderness. While he only had a window of maybe two months before the snows came, if he could force the Tsar's army into a pitched battle he knew he could land a war-winning knockout blow. Obliging him in this was the Russian commander-in-chief General Mikhail Kutuzov, pressured to fight for the Motherland's honor and kick the invaders out. He fortified the town of Borodino and awaited Napoleon's arrival, which came on September 7.

The resulting Battle of Borodino was the bloodiest single day of combat in the entirety of the Napoleonic Wars. At least 70,000 casualties resulted from the battle, with the number probably closer to 100,000 (as a point of reference, the bloodiest single day in American history was the Battle of Antietam during the Civil War, with just over 22,000 casualties). Unlike the deadly dance of parry and riposte at Austerlitz and Jena, Napoleon showed none of his tactical brilliance at Borodino. Units attacked entrenched Russian positions in massive human wave assaults, presaging the carnage of World War I by nearly a hundred years.

After almost ten straight hours of repelling French attacks, the defending Russians were beat up, exhausted, and low on ammunition. The decisive moment of the battle had arrived, the time when "a single drop of water causes overflow" as Napoleon described it. His generals urged him to commit the elite troops of his Imperial Guard to the battle, which he had been holding in reserve (this was actually typical for the Guard; although composed of the finest troops in the Empire, they were mostly kept as exquisitely dressed display pieces whose primary job was mop-up duty). Cementing in place one of history's greatest 'What Ifs,' Napoleon adamantly refused to send the Guard into combat. He had already won the battle, so why risk having his best troops, as he stated, "blown up?" By being too cautious, the famous gambler let his opportunity to destroy the Russian army slip away. Kutuzov withdrew his battered, yet intact, forces under cover of dark, opening the way to Moscow.

Although the French remained in possession of the field of corpses at the end of the day, the tremendous losses from the battle broke the back of the *Grande Armée.* Napoleon pushed his exhausted men on ahead to Moscow, believing that the fall of his capital would force the Tsar to capitulate. On September 14, French troops entered Moscow, but rather than a triumphal entry into the 'Third Rome,' they were greeted to a ghost town. The military had ordered the evacuation of the city several days prior and stripped it bare of any supplies the French might use. That night a great fire swept through the mostly wooden city and burned it to the ground. One can't help but imagine the conquering General surrounded by his Empire of Ashes, the meager remnants of his once *Grande Armeé* starving and freezing all around him.

After receiving no offer of peace by mid-October, Napoleon ordered the retreat from Moscow. Winter was coming, and the burned out capital surrounded by fields of desolation was no place to quarter an army. Thus began the long, humiliating retreat from Russia, as the French army, already reduced to just 100,000 men, seemed to shed troops by the kilometer. Rampant disease, hypothermia, starvation, and persistent Russian attacks turned the retreat into an unimaginable hell.

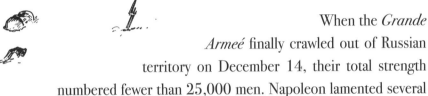

When the *Grande Armeé* finally crawled out of Russian territory on December 14, their total strength numbered fewer than 25,000 men. Napoleon lamented several times during his exile at St. Helena: "I should have died at Moscow."

XIV

NAPOLEON'S DOWNFALL:

THE END OF THE EMPIRE

AND THE HUNDRED DAYS

fter Napoleon traipsed back from Russia in defeat, his erstwhile allies saw their opportunity to strike and took it. Prussia, Austria, and Sweden all quickly broke their alliances with France and joined in with Great Britain and Russia to gang up on the Emperor while he was on the ropes. Their mad dash to turn on him at the first sniff of blood is ultimately a testament to Napoleon's utter failure as a diplomat. He might have crushed them repeatedly on the battlefield, but he committed an error common to war winners throughout history – he neither completely destroyed their ability to fight nor completely reconciled with them, but rather left them in a state of weakened, indignant humiliation.

On the home front, the French people were exhausted and the Empire's formidable resources nearly tapped out. In December of 1812, there was even a coup attempt in Paris, something that would have been unimaginable a year earlier. These domestic strains make it all the more impressive that Napoleon was able to raise nearly another 600,000 troops over the winter and spring of 1813. Although formidable, these forces were spread thin fighting a two-front war against Britain, Spain, and Portugal in the Pyrenees, and Prussia, Austria, Russia, and Sweden in Germany. On October 16-19, Napoleon's French/Polish/Italian army of approximately 200,000 troops faced off against the Russian/Austrian/Prussian/Swedish army of nearly 400,000 at the Battle of Leipzig, also known as the Battle of Nations (for obvious reasons). In this, the largest battle ever fought in Europe (only to be surpassed during World War I), Napoleon suffered his first-ever decisive defeat.

With the loss at Leipzig, the Grand Empire started to collapse as the Coalition abolished the Napoleonic satellite states of the Grand Duchy of Warsaw, Confederation of the Rhine, and Kingdom of Italy. In early 1814, they pressed their advantage and invaded France proper, leaving Napoleon to scrounge together whatever forces he could for a desperate defense of the homeland. While horribly outmanned and outgunned, the dire situation reignited a fire long dormant in the general. The legend returned, and he fought perhaps the greatest campaign of his career. In four days he won four separate battles, inflicting 18,000 casualties while only suffering 3,000, despite being outnumbered 4-1. However, in spite of these unlikely victories, the Coalition could afford to replace their losses while Napoleon could not. On March 30, Paris fell, but the still-defiant Napoleon dreamed of uniting his disparate forces for a final epic battle in the capital itself. However, his marshals refused and told their Emperor that they would not throw their men's lives away. With no other choice left, on April 11, 1814, Napoleon signed the Treaty of Fontainebleau, abdicating his position as emperor and agreeing to go into exile on the tiny island of Elba off the coast of Tuscany. On May 3, 1814, he arrived in his new truncated kingdom with a military retinue of three hundred men. The poetic justice of the situation for the island boy turned emperor was unmistakable.

Over the next several months, as Napoleon mobilized his new Elban subjects into building roads, clearing forests, and blasting mines, representatives of the victorious powers met at Vienna to redraw the map of Europe.

The Congress of Vienna would last into the summer of 1815, and was the world's first multi-national conference of Great Powers, being the forerunner of future bodies such as the League of Nations, United Nations, and NATO. After more than two decades of continual war, the Congress' job was create a stable international regime that would assure lasting peace and redraw ancient borders since rendered obsolete.

One of the Congress' first acts was to formalize the decision of the Great Powers to restore the Bourbon Monarchy to France, installing Louis XVI's younger brother, the Count of Provence, as the new king. So here we are – after twenty-five years of revolution, mob violence, royal executions, assemblies, conventions, rotating door constitutions, terrors, cults, republics, and military dictatorships – right back at where we started, with King Louis on the throne of France. However, in an implicit concession to the Revolution's permanency, the Great Powers made

Louis XVIII's ascension to the throne contingent on his granting a constitution, establishing a bicameral legislature and guaranteeing freedom of speech, the press, religion, and private property. Even the Napoleonic code would remain in its entirety along with his educational and social reforms. The king had returned for sure, but not in a way recognizable to the royalists of 1789.

While initially popular for granting a rather liberal constitution, Louis' traditionalist impulses quickly turned public opinion (a truly revolutionary invention if there ever was one) sharply against him. The *émigré* nobility returned and quickly found their place back into the royal court. Roman Catholicism was re-established as the state religion. Trappings of the *ancien régime* returned, such as the white royalist flag replacing the republican tricolor. Perhaps the biggest gripe against 'Louis the Large' (he reportedly weighed in excess of 300 lbs.) was that he appeared to be a figurehead, foisted on the nation by foreign powers to keep her docile and pliant.

Meanwhile, without the unifying existential threat of the Corsican Ogre at their doorstep, the Great Powers soon fell into bickering over who should get what at the Congress of Vienna.

Russia wanted all of Poland, but Prussia thought they should divide it between themselves. Prussia pushed for all of Saxony, whereas Austria feared Prussia's rising power in Germany and blocked the move. Austria wanted all her former territories in Italy returned to her without giving up anything in return. Only the work of Lord Castlereagh of the United Kingdom and the born-again monarchist Talleyrand of France (famously described by Napoleon as "shit in a silk stocking") prevented war from breaking out amongst the Continental powers.

Tallyrand

All this news reached Napoleon on Elba, and the "tiger in the badly latched cage" saw his moment to pounce. On the night of February 26, 1815, he took a small ship with several hundred loyal troops and landed in Golfe-Juan near Antibes in southern France. The events to follow seem more written for a movie script than actual history. Napoleon only had a small honor guard with him and no assurance that he wouldn't be shot on sight. He had to rely on the force of his personality to rally the people to his cause and hope the memory of his glorious victories remained in the forefront of their minds. Once again, his gamble paid off and former soldiers flocked to his banner. His handful of men grew into thousands when the Fifth Line Regiment defected to Napoleon on March 7 after he flung open his coat to his would-be captors and shouted, "If any of you would kill his Emperor, here I stand!" As Napoleon continued his march towards Paris and his ranks swelled into an army, a panicked Louis XVIII dispatched one of his most capable generals with a full division of troops. The former Napoleonic commander, Michel Ney, boasted to the King that he would bring Napoleon back to Paris in an iron cage. However, when the marshal came face to face with his Emperor, he turned over his troops and pledged his service. Louis was left with little choice but to flee the country again and hope that the Coalition would be able to return him to power.

During his last years, Napoleon would reminisce on this triumphant return from exile (known as the Hundred Days) as the happiest time of his life. He entered Paris to much fanfare on March 20, and set about rebuilding the Empire on a more liberal model. He abolished press censorship and gave real power to a freely elected parliament. It's probably impossible to know whether Napoleon had a real change of heart or if this was just another pragmatic move to rally as much support around his regime as possible, but the short lived model of this 'Liberal Empire' would rally future Bonapartists for the next hundred years. He was able to pay little attention to governing, however, after the Coalition Powers agreed on March 25 to declare Napoleon an outlaw and never rest until they removed him from power permanently.

Napoleon's only hope of keeping his throne was to defeat several of the Coalition armies piecemeal and force them to the peace table. The closest force was the English army in Belgium. If Napoleon could crush them there, then he could defeat the Prussian army marching to reinforce them, before turning south towards the Austro-Russian army in Germany. It was a longshot, but so was a Corsican artilleryman becoming Emperor of the French.

Following several small engagements, Napoleon finally met up with the English army commanded by his old scourge, the Duke of Wellington, near the village of Waterloo on June 18. In this grand finale to the Napoleonic Wars, French troops crashed repeatedly against English lines, which refused to break. As the Prussian reinforcements began to arrive late in the day, Napoleon knew he needed a bold stroke that would either win or lose the battle for him. Unlike at Borodino when he held the Imperial Guard in reserve, this time he committed them in one last glorious charge to break the British center. As the sun set on the battlefield of Waterloo, the undefeated Guard divisions came under intense musket and artillery fire. Several regiments were slaughtered to a man, famously replying when offered quarter, "The Guard dies, it does not surrender!" After coming under a vicious bayonet charge by British grenadiers, the remnants of the shattered Imperial Guard broke off their attack. Word of the most elite unit in the entire French army sounding the retreat sent a panic through the rest of the French army: *"La Garde recule! Sauve qui peut!"* ("The Guard retreats! Save yourself if you can!"). Panic turned into rout, as French troops began to flee the field. The battle was over, and with it Napoleon's long and illustrious career.

While he did not want to give up fighting, his support in Paris quickly melted away. Enough was enough, they had stuck with him through Waterloo, but now his final defeat was inevitable. Their thoughts turned to saving their own skins by condemning the Emperor and delivering him into Coalition hands. Napoleon agreed to abdicate, again, but with one condition: they declare his four-year-old son Emperor as 'Napoleon II.' It would matter little since the Coalition powers refused to recognize Napoleon the Younger as emperor, slapping the title Duke of Reichstadt on him and shipping him off to live with his grandfather the Emperor of Austria (he would later die of tuberculosis at the age of 21).

With all of Europe on his tail, Napoleon raced for the coast, hoping to catch a ship bound for New York before the Coalition could catch up to him. His brothers Joseph, Lucien, and Jerome all planned to meet up with him in America where they could rally support for a third Napoleonic sequel. It was not to be; the British got wind of his plans and blockaded the ports. With no hope of escape remaining, Napoleon surrendered himself to Captain Maitland of the *HMS Bellerophon* on July 15, 1815. He was exiled once again, only this time to the British island of St. Helena in the middle of the Atlantic Ocean. There he would stay for the six years remaining of his life, quietly writing his memoirs and pondering what could have been.

BONAPARTES
IN AMERICA

While Napoleon never made it across the Atlantic, other members of his family did manage to leave a Bonapartist imprint on America. His older brother Joseph, the ex-king of Spain and Naples, was smuggled out of Europe aboard the American ship *Commerce* in 1815. Upon arrival in the United States, he lived for a time in hotels in New York City and Philadelphia before purchasing the estate of Point Breeze in Bordentown, New Jersey, with the few Spanish crown jewels he managed to take with him. By all accounts, he enjoyed a quiet and genteel retirement for the next 25 years, entertaining elite American and European guests in his pseudo-regal estate. Since his wife did not accompany him, Joseph took a mistress and had two daughters with her. He also reported a hunting encounter with the legendary Jersey Devil, and thereafter obsessed about killing it and bringing the stuffed monster back to Europe as a trophy. Napoleon's younger brother, Jerome, came to the United States in the early 1800s and married Baltimore socialite Elisabeth Patterson with whom he had a son, also named Jerome. While a furious Napoleon quickly dissolved the marriage, the idea of an American Bonaparte dynasty so terrified Congress that they passed a Titles of Nobility Amendment to the Constitution, stripping citizenship from anyone accepting a noble title from a foreign power (it was never ratified). Both of Jerome's American grandchildren did well for themselves. Jerome Napoleon Bonaparte II graduated from West Point and served in the U.S. army before joining the French army under his cousin Napoleon III. His brother Charles Bonaparte went to Harvard Law School and served as U.S. Secretary of the Navy and later Attorney General under President Theodore Roosevelt, where he created the forerunner to the FBI. Today, the head of House Bonaparte and claimant to the Imperial French Crown, Jean-Christophe (also a descendant of Jerome), lives in New York and London, where he works in private equity – a profession only slightly more hated than world-conquering dictator.

XV

TURNING BACK THE CLOCK

ON THE REVOLUTION:

THE CONGRESS OF VIENNA

AND BOURBON RESTORATION

Just one week prior to the Battle of Waterloo, the Congress of Vienna wrapped up its work establishing the new European order. Curiously, this new order looked a lot like the old order prior to 1789. They reaffirmed the monarchial principle over the republican one, refuting the ideals of the Revolution as injurious to peace. Their goal was to create a balance of power in Europe, where-by no single country could dominate any other. This new Conservative Order was no doubt reactionary and set back the cause of liberal-ism in Europe by a generation, but it did have one undeniable achievement. The international regime that emerged from the Congress of Vienna prevented the outbreak of another general European war for nearly a century, until World War I shattered it in 1914.

Try as they might, there was no simply no way to put the genie back in the bottle after twenty-five years of revolution. In order to survive as long as it did, the *ancien régime* had depended on continuity. The Revolution broke that continuity and scrubbed away the patina of mystique surrounding dynastic monarchy. Memories of rights and freedoms obtained and then lost don't just disappear from the public mind, and Napoleon's modern conception of the secular, national state was not as easy to exile from Europe as the man himself. Louis XVIII occupied the throne once again, but he never sat upon it with the ease that his ancestors did. His rule was no longer an immutable law of nature like gravity, but rather something permissive, subject to the changing whims of popular opinion. The man deserves some credit for understanding this shift. After returning from a second exile, Louis moderated his views and accepted his role as a constitutional monarch.

The King's first political challenge was to deal with the far-right Chamber of Deputies, dominated by an extreme conservative party known as the Ultra-Royalists, or 'Ultras' for short. Elected in the chaotic aftermath of the Hundred Days, pro-royalist groups throughout France orchestrated a new White Terror to bully the population into voting for their candidates. Both Louis XVIII and Talleyrand hoped for a moderate (and pliable) Chamber, but instead they ended up with a majority of conservative ideologues not at all representative of the country at large. Dubbed the *"chambre introuvable"* (unobtainable chamber) by the King for their hardline stance on rolling back everything that had happened since 1789, the Ultras had the reputation for being *"plus royaliste que le Roi"* (more royalist than the King). With tensions escalating between the Ultras and the Crown, the conservative deputies refused to fund the government in 1816, unless the King gave in to their demands. Louis had had enough. Rather than be blackmailed, he invoked his royal prerogative and dissolved the chamber, calling for new elections. To ensure a favorable result, he expanded the franchise and ger-rymandered districts to ensure more liberals were elected to the Chamber of Deputies. The effort was a success, bringing the *Doctrinaires* to power, a center-left party that tried to reconcile a constitutional monarchy with the gains of the Revolution. The *Doctrinaires* would keep their majority in the Chamber until 1820.

Louis never had any children, so his younger brother and well-known Ultra, the Count of Artois, remained next in the line of succession. On February 13, 1820, a radical Bonapartist assassinated the Count of Artois's younger son and fellow Ultra, the Duke of Berry. While there was no direct link between the assassin and the *Doctrinaires,* the Ultras used it as a campaign issue and re-captured their majority in the legislature. Led by Villèle, the new Ultra-dominated Chamber moderated their reactionary tendencies and waited Louis out, hoping to remain in power long enough for nature to take care of the morbidly obese king. It did not take long. On April 16, 1824, Louis XVIII died of gout and gangrene caused by his massive girth. He would be the last king of France to die while reigning. His slim, athletic, and staunchly conservative brother succeeded him, taking the regnal name Charles X. For the first time, the Ultra-Royalists controlled both the Chamber of Deputies and the Throne, opening the way for a full reinstatement of the *ancien régime.*

Unlike Louis XVIII who accepted the need to reign as a limited, con-stitutional monarch in order to remain on the throne, Charles X suffered no such limit to his authority. As Charles saw it, the revolutionary interlude was but a brief blip of civil unrest in the thousand-year history of the French monarchy. It was a revolt against the legitimate government, albeit a dis-turbingly lengthy and successful one mind you, but still just a revolt and nothing more. To make any concessions to revolutionary ideas of 'progress' was to concede the point. Charles refused to reconcile his reign with the legacy of the French Revolution. Instead, he did everything in his power to wipe away everything that came after 1789.

Nobles and clergy who had their lands confiscated during the Revolution were compensated for that loss at public expense, costing the State nearly a billion francs. In January of 1825, his Ultra-Royalist Chamber passed the deeply reactionary Anti-Sacrilege Act, which made various forms of blasphemy and sacrilege punishable by death. It is not hard to see that Charles X did not exactly endear himself to his subjects. Oblivious to popular perception of his actions, he arranged a full-blown royal coronation at Reims Cathedral – which Louis XVIII had decided to forego. Girded with the sword of Charlemagne and anointed by the Archbishop with sacred oil from the Holy Ampulla (allegedly descended from Heaven to anoint Clovis I, the first Christian king of France) everything about the ceremony was designed to loudly pronounce: The Revolution is dead, long live the King! As his *pièce de résistance,* Charles revived the ancient practice of laying on hands after the coronation, believing that the royal touch could cure the sick of their illnesses.

Public opinion of Charles and the Ultras continued to deteriorate throughout the latter half of the 1820's. An economic downturn further alienated the increasingly influential business community, who blamed the regime for their retrograde policies. Rather than moderate his views and compromise with the opposition, Charles became increasingly hardline and surrounded himself exclusively with other Ultras. Villèle knew the government needed to do something to rally support behind it, and what better way to distract from problems at home than to launch a war against a weak Muslim neighbor? Citing ongoing piracy in the Mediterranean and a diplomatic insult by the Dey of Algiers (he hit the French ambassador with his fan after the man dodged questions concerning repayment of delinquent war debts), Charles X ordered an invasion to 'pacify' the country in June of 1830. French troops landed in Algeria on June 14, and they literally rocked the Kasbah of Algiers on July 7, sending the Dey into exile. The invasion of Algeria was Charles' only policy decision that lasted beyond his reign. For the next 130 years, France would maintain a colonial presence in Algeria, only ending in 1962 after a bloody war for independence, the scars of which remain today.

Charles X never got a chance to bask in military glory however. In spite of efforts to manipulate the electoral results, the returns in 1830 were a sharp rebuke to the Ultra-Royalist administration. For the first time in his reign, Charles' would have to contend with a liberal Chamber of Deputies, something he was not prepared to accept. Invoking a special clause in the constitution, the King declared a national emergency and assumed absolute control over the government. On July 25, he promulgated the July Ordinances, dissolving the Chamber of Deputies, suspending freedom of the press, and stripping the franchise from most of the bourgeoisie. Charles had finally done what Louis XVIII had feared – show his hand as a neo-absolutist and unite the entire opposition against him. For the first time in twenty-five years, the tricolor flag went up all over Paris and *La Marseillaise* rang out again. When the King asked whether there was a revolt breaking out in his capital, one of his marshals replied, "No sire, it is not a revolt, but a revolution."

For the next three days, known as the *Trois Glorieuses* (Three Glorious Days), the long dormant Revolution returned to the streets of Paris. It is this Revolution of 1830, not its better-known 1789 coun-

terpart, that Eugène Delacroix depicted in his famous painting, *Liberty
Leading the People.* Liberal newspapers such as *Le National* published a
call to revolt, with famous journalists

such as Adolphe Thiers (we will see him again soon) proclaiming: "The
legal regime has been interrupted . . . Obedience ceases to be a duty!" While
the royal troops fought bravely, the sheer weight of numbers overwhelmed
them. As July 29 dawned, most of Paris was under the control of the revolutionaries. They had erected over 4,000 barricades to block passage of royal
troops through the city streets and by noon of that day the most important
buildings – the Tuileries, the Louvre, the Palais de Justice, and the Hôtel
de Ville – all had the tricolor banner flying overhead. Upon learning of this,
Talleyrand declared, "Take note that on July 29, 1830, at five minutes past
twelve o'clock, the elder branch of the Bourbons ceased to reign."

With the few remaining troops loyal to him, Charles X departed for the
safety of Versailles, leaving his cousin Louis-Philippe in charge. With no
other options remaining to him, on August 2, 1830, Charles X abdicated

the throne in favor of his grandson, Henri. Rather than proclaim the young child King Henri V as instructed, Louis-Philippe saw the opportunity to seize the throne for himself and stood by silently as the Chamber of Deputies debated what to do next. Charles and his family had already fled across the Channel to England, whereas Louis-Philippe stayed in Paris and helped restore order to the capital. The businessmen making up most of the Chamber believed they had a friend in the outspoken liberal Louis-Philippe, and offered him the throne if he swore to govern as a constitutional monarch – an offer he gladly accepted.

On August 7, the Chamber approved the Charter of 1830 as a compromise between royalism and republicanism. Louis-Philippe would receive the title 'King of the French' based on the principle of popular sovereignty rather than divine right. It curtailed the king's powers while expanding the franchise to include a broader swath of the population. Titles of nobility were once again abolished, and freedoms of speech, the press, religion, and assembly were all guaranteed. Two days later, surrounded by tricolor flags, Louis-Philippe swore an oath before the assembled Chamber of Deputies and National Guard to rule based on the will of the people, inaugurating the period of the July Monarchy.

CHARTE
CONSTITUTIONNELLE
1830

XVI

THE BOYS OF SUMMER:
LOUIS-PHILIPPE
AND THE JULY MONARCHY

Who was this new progressive king who appeared seemingly out of nowhere? Louis-Philippe belonged to the House of Orléans, a cadet branch to the senior House of Bourbon. While related, the two noble houses were more often rivals than allies. House Bourbon, perhaps because it was actually in charge, was more stodgy and conservative, whereas House Orléans had a reputation for being more open to change and new ideas. Louis-Philippe's father, the Duke of Orléans, was the most high-profile nobleman to support the Revolution back in its early days, even turning his Parisian residence, the opulent Palais-Royal, into a meeting place for revolutionary agitators. After he changed his name to Philippe Égalité and voted for Louis XVI's death, the royalists never forgave him or his house for this betrayal.

During the French Revolutionary Wars, the young Louis-Philippe led troops on the frontier, fighting with distinction at the battles of Valmy and Jemappes. Showing more foresight than his father, when General Dumouriez defected to the Austrian camp, Louis-Philippe joined him. Surrounded by a hostile Europe, he booked passage across the Atlantic to seek refuge in the United States. For four years, he moved throughout the country, living in Philadelphia with his brothers, in an apartment on 75th and Broadway in New York, and in downtown Boston, where he rented a room above the Union Oyster House and tutored students in French. Like Alexis de Tocqueville and Lafayette before him, the new nation impressed Louis-Philippe and he wished to incorporate America's aptitude for business into French society.

It's not surprising that the strongest supporters of his regime were big business. You can almost see the shift from *ancien régime* to post-revolutionary kingship here. While Charles X had aristocrats and bishops as his core supporters, Louis-Philippe's base consisted of bankers and merchants. The bourgeoisie may have loved him, but the 'Citizen King' never was a hit with the lower classes who saw him as a sell-out. They were the ones who spilled their blood in the Revolution of 1830 to put Louis-Philippe on the throne. If Louis-Philippe now chose to surround himself with rich fat cats while ignoring the pleas of the common man, then they would show him how necessary their support was.

In 1832, a cholera epidemic swept through Paris and took the life of popular leftist general Jean Lamarque. Republican partisans and the disaffected urban poor used his funeral as an opportunity to protest against government policies favoring the rich. As tends to happen when a large group of agitated people get together, the rhetoric became more heated and eventually lead to violence between the protestors and government troops. Homes in friendly working class districts unfurled red banners with the words 'Liberty or Death,' even throwing down furniture from the windows

FURNITURE FOR YOUR BARRICADE

to help the protestors construct barricades. By nightfall, over 3,000 protestors occupied the eastern third of Paris and called for a full insurrection
the next day.

As anyone who has seen *Les Misérables* can attest, the revolt didn't
end well. The expected uprising from the rest of Paris never came, and the
superior numbers and firepower of the government troops soon overwhelmed
the 3,000 or so insurrectionists. While Louis-Philippe's quick response
allowed him to avoid the fate of his exiled cousin Charles X, his popularity
never recovered from this incident. It's hard to maintain credibility as a
Citizen King when you rely on bloody bayonets to support your throne.

The memory of this failed Paris Uprising of 1832 remained a bitter pill
for the working classes and united them against the regime. It is during the
reign of Louis-Philippe that the primary social struggle in France changed
from one between orders (i.e., the nobility and clergy versus the Third
Estate) to one between classes. The bourgeoisie-dominated government
saw that industry was the future, so they provided generous subsidies for
firms to build factories, railroads, and steam-powered ships. The industrial
revolution had finally come to France in full force, and with its many
benefits came all the attendant social ills. Poor farmers flocked from the
countryside into the cities looking for work, creating densely packed and
unsanitary urban slums. The working day routinely topped fourteen hours
of backbreaking labor in dangerous conditions. The only relief passed under
Prime Minister Adolphe Thiers, who had moved considerably to the right
since his *Le National* days (marrying a rich heiress will do such things), was
a meager child labor law, restricting dangerous factory work for children
under the age of eight and nighttime work for those under age thirteen.

These policies became more intolerable after the conservative and
eminently quotable minister François Guizot replaced Thiers. An opponent
of republicanism, he coined the phrase later reworked and made famous by
Winston Churchill: "Not to be a republican at twenty is proof of want of
heart; to be one at thirty is proof of want of head." Justifying his actions
as a means to prevent future uprisings, Guizot banned all forms of public

assembly, including political clubs and labor unions. While he did increase government funding for education and ensure that every French commune had at least one public primary school, he fiercely opposed any attempt to extend voting rights beyond wealthy males. When a heckler shouted at Guizot during a rally that he wanted the right to vote, Guizot famously replied, "Enrich yourself, then you'll be able to vote!"

The bourgeoisie took his advice and enriched themselves immensely as industry expanded. In 1838, Paris' first department store, Le Bon Marché, opened, displaying its upscale consumer goods for all to see (in case you were wondering, it's still there and still ritzy, currently owned by luxury goods conglomerate LVMH). Unlike under the old regime when wealthy nobles and bishops mostly kept to their chateaux in the countryside, now the inequality gap was visible and notorious on the streets of Paris. The growing divide between rich and poor created obvious resentment, while the rapid changes sweeping through French society lead to a new breed of *philosophe,* dedicated to rethinking how politics and economics should operate.

These early utopian socialists didn't share a cohesive ideology, but they all believed that the industrial revolution was a civilizational game changer. In a sense, they were right. It was only in the 19th century that the standard of living for an average French peasant equaled that of a Roman citizen living 2,000 years prior. Terms such as economic growth simply did not exist; people expected just to farm and get by. By the 1830s and 40s, industrialization brought material abundance seemingly out of nowhere, but the rewards of that abundance overwhelmingly went to a small slice of the population. Shouldn't all people have the opportunity to contribute and share in industry's plentiful fruits?

Aristocrat-turned-socialist Henri Saint-Simon imagined a harmonious society modeled after Plato's *Republic*, where the educated ruled based on scientific principles and the State guaranteed work and sustenance to all according to their skills. Charles Fourier had a more radical view, advocating for the creation of massive 'grand hotels' he called *phalanstères* to house independent worker's communes. Each *phalanstère* would be wholly self-sufficient (pre-dating the 20th century concept of arcologies) and in Fourier's vision, millions of these *phalanstères* would dot the globe, loosely governed by a World Congress. On the less utopian end of the spectrum was the militant Louis Blanqui, who advocated a violent overthrow of the existing order. Karl Marx himself spent several years in Paris (from 1843 until 1845 when Guizot finally kicked him out), where he met Friedrich Engels at the Café de la Régence. It was during these two years that he familiarized himself with the works of British economists Adam Smith and David Ricardo along with those of the French utopian socialists. Marx drew these disparate sources together to develop his own cohesive doctrine of Communism, which he fully detailed several decades later in his magnum opus *Das Kapital*.

As the public continued to sour on the July Monarchy, the regime attempted various publicity stunts to bolster their flagging support. In 1840, after much debate, Louis-Philippe approved the exhumation of Napoleon's remains from St. Helena's and their triumphal return to France. Intended to reconcile the July Monarchy with both the Revolution and the

First Empire (and perhaps scrape off a little residual glory for itself), the grandiose ceremony of the *Retour des Cendres* (Return of the Ashes) had the opposite effect, reminding the people of how far they had fallen. Both the optimism of the Republic and the glory of the Empire were gone, replaced by the bland rule of bankers and their prosaic trouser wearing king.

King Louis Phillippe "Le Poire"

(KUDOS TO PHILIPON, DAUMIER, + TUBIR COMPATRIOTS)

The harvest of 1846 was historically bad across the Continent, but hit the French economy particularly hard. Unemployment skyrocketed and workers demonstrated across the country; an estimated 1 in 3 Parisian families were forced onto the welfare rolls. In an attempt to appeal to the left, Louis-Philippe replaced Guizot with Thiers as his prime minister, but the government's stance towards popular demonstrations only grew more repressive. With public meetings banned, political organizations used civic festivals as a way to get around the law. In 1847, the left organized a 'banquet campaign' in several cities throughout France, holding banquets (otherwise permitted, this is France after all) as a pretext for political meetings. The government quickly caught wind of what was going on and took the step that proved to be their undoing – they banned the banquet. When word reached Paris on February 22, 1848, a mass riot broke out and barricades went up in working-class districts all over the city yet again. After an eighteen-year interlude, the French Revolution was back.

THE PRINCE OF PARIS AND THE CIVIL WAR

While he would never become king, Louis-Philippe's grandson, Prince Philippe, did serve for a year as an officer in the Union Army during the Civil War. As an exiled royal with ambitions to one day regain the throne, Prince Philippe needed to keep his name in the news and burnish his Orléanist credentials as a progressive constitutional monarchist. He also desired military experience and was curious to see if democratic government could survive in America. General George McClellan, commander of the Army of the Potomac, welcomed such a prestigious guest into his camp and invited him to join his personal staff as aide-de-camp. During his time with the army, Prince Philippe kept a lengthy journal where he documented the conditions in the camp, the relationships between various high-ranking officers and policy makers in the government, and the failure of the Union Army to capture the Confederate capital of Richmond during the Peninsular Campaign. As concerns about Britain and France intervening in the war increased in 1862, the Prince voluntarily resigned his commission to avoid a diplomatic incident. He did have a real chance of becoming king after the Second Empire collapsed in 1870, but his unpopular cousin Henri (Charles X's oldest son) had a stronger claim to the throne and sabotaged any hopes of another restoration when he refused to recognize the tricolor as France's official flag. By the time Henri died in 1883, it was too late for Philippe. The Third Republic had been in existence for more than 10 years and people had little appetite to restore the monarchy yet again.

art: "Philippe d'Orleans Comte de Paris 1862" by Mathew Brady
Licensed under Public domain via Wikimedia Commons.

XVII

FRENCH REVOLUTION OF 1848

AND THE SECOND REPUBLIC:

WHAT HAPPENS WHEN YOU RUN OUT

OF KINGS TO OVERTHROW

The year 1848 was marked by revolutions throughout Europe, as if all the pent-up liberalism of the past thirty-five years had suddenly burst forth from the post Congress of Vienna conservative consensus. While revolts in Prussia, Austria, Poland, Italy, and Ireland were all violently suppressed, the French revolutionaries succeeded in toppling their government once again. The Revolution of 1848 was nearly a complete replay of the Revolution of 1830. After some initial bloodshed, the National Guard went over to the revolutionaries and in only three days, all of Paris was under their control. Just like his cousin Charles X, Louis-Philippe abdicated in favor of his grandson (whom everybody promptly ignored) and fled across the Channel to a life of genteel exile in England. On February 26, 1848, a provisional government in Paris declared the monarchy abolished yet again. For the first time since

Napoleon's rise to power, France was a republic once again.

From its inception, the Second Republic was a government divided against itself. Having achieved their goal of ousting Louis-Philippe, the leaders of the new regime split between old school republicans who pined for a restoration of the First Republic, and radical republicans who wished to transform France into a 'Democratic and Social Republic.' These two dueling factions organized themselves into a National Assembly along the lines of the old model, and scheduled elections based on universal male suffrage. It was the responsibility of the newly elected Assembly to create a fresh constitution for the new Republic.

In the interim, left-wing Parisian delegates dominated the National Assembly and worked quickly to enact the legislation they wanted prior to election season. At the top of their platform was a right to work law, whereby the State would guarantee a job to all unemployed citizens. To effectuate this, the socialist-dominated Assembly authorized the creation of 'national workshops' in Paris to provide jobs to the unemployed. Over the coming months, thousands of out-of-work laborers flocked to the capital, overloading the system. Without sufficient jobs in the national workshops to accommodate everybody, the government employed laborers in public works projects like road and railway construction, and when even that proved inadequate, they plugged them in make-work positions like digging ditches and filling them back in again. While this might have thrilled the hard-up urban proletariat, it alienated the bourgeoisie and rural farmers who saw their taxes increase to pay for this expansion of social services.

The election returns proved highly unfavorable for the socialists, as most of the country (at least outside of the big cities) voted for the conservative 'Party of Order.' Tensions mounted, and in May, an armed mob led by Louis Blanqui attempted to overthrow the Assembly and establish a Worker's Republic. The bourgeoisie-dominated National Guard came to the Assembly's defense and put the mob down. The battle lines over the soul of the new Republic could not be clearer. On June 21, the Assembly issued a decree announcing the closure of the national workshops in three days. All able-bodied men would be offered the choice to enlist in the army or face immediate termination. Faced with the choice of destitution or military service, the swollen Parisian workforce raised the red flag on June 23, taking to the streets. Over the coming days, their numbers swelled to forty, then sixty, then eighty thousand, and continued to grow into six figures. Had the long simmering socialist revolution finally come to France? General Cavaignac called in active duty army units along with the National Guard, until over 130,000 government troops stormed the streets of Paris. For three days fighting raged throughout the City of Lights, as government forces and socialist revolutionaries engaged in a fight to the death. On June 26, the shooting stopped; 10,000 casualties later, the army had won. The failure of the June Days Uprising destroyed the radicals and their hopes for a Democratic and Social Republic.

The new constitution went into effect on November 4, 1848. Unlike earlier attempts to model their government on legislatively focused parliamentary systems, this time the French opted for an executive focused presidential system. Similar to the American Presidency, the President of France would act as both Head of Government and Head of State, serving as Commander-in-Chief of the military. In the first presidential election in French history, three candidates rose to the fore: the conservative General Louis-Eugène Cavaignac, the socialist Alexandre Auguste Ledru-Rollin, and the moderate Louis-Napoleon Bonaparte. Louis-Napoleon won in a landslide, capturing over 75% of the vote across all segments of the electorate. Thirty-three years after Napoleon's exile to St. Helena, a Bonaparte was in charge of France once again.

The new President-elect was the youngest son of Louis Bonaparte, brother of the Emperor Napoleon (who acted as his godfather). After the fall of the Empire, Louis-Napoleon fled the country along with the rest of the Bonaparte dynasty, and grew up in Switzerland, Germany, and Italy. While in exile, Louis-Napoleon refined his uncle's political beliefs into a semi-coherent philosophy of 'Bonapartism,' whereby a strong leader, ruling over a highly centralized state, acted with the consent of the people for the benefit of the nation as a whole. Like seemingly all French exiles at the time, he lived for a period in both New York and London, where he developed an admiration for Anglo-American industry.

In a quixotic attempt to repeat Napoleon's Hundred Days, he landed at the port of Boulogne with sixty loyal supporters back in August 6, 1840, expecting the garrison to flock to his cause against the unpopular Louis-Philippe. Instead, he was quickly arrested, tried, and given a life sentence for his botched coup. After six years of incarceration,

Louis-Napoleon's doctor helped him to escape. He fled back across the Channel to London as a shrewder man. This time he would wait for a good opportunity to present itself before he attempted to seize power again. The fall of the July Monarchy and establishment of the Second Republic proved to be just that opportunity.

Much like his uncle, Louis-Napoleon's political strategy revolved around playing both sides against the middle. In a world where the left advocated socialist revolution and the right was split between another restoration of the stale monarchy or rule by the ultra-rich, Louis-Napoleon could easily position himself as the moderate choice opposing both partisan extremes. The failed July Days Uprising did major damage to the left's image and led to the election of a very conservative legislature in 1849. With one flank secure, Louis-Napoleon turned his guns on the right-wing dominated Assembly, led now by former liberal Adolphe Thiers. Gridlock and confrontation characterized the relationship between the President and the Assembly for the next two years. Each side tried to run out the clock on the other – the President believing that it was just a matter of time until the conservatives in the Assembly shot themselves in the foot, and the Assembly knowing Louis-Napoleon's position was term limited to 1852.

Louis-Napoleon was wildly popular – especially among the French peasantry who rallied behind the name Bonaparte – and had no intention of stepping down in 1852. He campaigned around the country in favor of amending the constitution to allow for presidential re-election, positioning himself as France's only bulwark against both Socialism and Monarchism. On May 31, 1850, a frightened Assembly gave Louis-Napoleon the political ammunition he needed – they changed the election laws to restrict voting to only those who met certain income requirements. By taking away the franchise from the "vile multitude" as Thiers called them, the Assembly allowed Louis-Napoleon to campaign on the platform of voting rights for all. Thiers, for his part, used all of his parliamentary muscle to create an Anti-Bonaparte alliance between the far left and far right in the Assembly, using the threat of Louis-Napoleon's second term to bring them together.

After repeated, failed attempts to get the Assembly to pass a universal suffrage law and amend the constitution, Louis-Napoleon decided he had the justification he needed to attempt his very own *coup d'état*. In less than subtle fashion, he set the date for his coup on the anniversary of his uncle's coronation, December 2, and named it "Operation Rubicon" in emulation of Julius Caesar. One can see why this event inspired Karl Marx to coin his famous quote, "History repeats itself, the first time as tragedy, then as farce." Farcical it may have been, but Louis-Napoleon's control over the military and the unpopularity of the Assembly ensured the coup's success. After some fighting in Paris and in loyal republican towns throughout France, all resistance ended by December 10.

XVIII

NAPOLEON III:

THE EMPIRE STRIKES BACK

Louis-Napoleon quickly consolidated his own power after the coup. First, to legitimize his military overthrow of the government, he relied once again on that favored tool of Bonapartism: the plebiscite. On December 22, over 92% of voters approved of Louis-Napoleon remaining on as president and authorized the drafting of a new constitution, which was speedily enacted only three weeks later on January 14, 1852. The Constitution of 1852 (I know, there seem to be more years with a constitution than without) formally enshrined Bonapartist ideology in a governing document, rejecting the monarchy of the old regime and restoration governments, while pledging fidelity to the "principles of 1789" best expressed in the First French Empire.

While the people remained sovereign, they would exercise this sovereignty by placing all governing authority in the hands of a single individual. Louis-Napoleon maintained the pretext of ruling as *Monsieur President* for the most of 1852, until finally popping the question of whether to elevate his position to that of Emperor in November. Once again, 97% of the electorate gave their approval, and on December 2, exactly one year after the coup, the Senate declared the French Empire restored, with President Louis-Napoleon Bonaparte becoming the Emperor Napoleon III.

Napoleon III knew his people well, and realized the nostalgia they held for the First Empire as the Camelot of its day. Unlike the regressive and class stratified monarchies or chaotic and bloody republics, the Empire represented order, prosperity, and glory. Napoleon III tapped into this desire for grandeur and promised to restore France's rightful place in Europe and the world as a Great Power. The 'Concert of Europe' established after the Congress of Vienna to keep the peace envisaged a weak and docile France.

Napoleon III needed to walk a tightrope by both asserting a more muscular foreign policy while also reassuring his nervous neighbors that he had no desire for aggressive war. The key seemed to be unthinkable, an alliance with France's oldest and most implacable enemy: England, perfidious Albion. The two countries had been engaged in a constant struggle since the outbreak of the Hundred Years War in 1337, and never looked back. However, to paraphrase from British Prime Minister Lord Palmerston, nations have no permanent friends or permanent enemies but only permanent interests, and it was in the interests of both England and France to draw together.

The best way to do this was by peeling Britain away from the Quadruple Alliance with Austria, Prussia, and Russia. Russia, in addition to being the strongest continental power, was also the most bellicose. As the once-great Ottoman Empire continued to decline, Russia took the opportunity to bully concessions out of her neighbor. Napoleon III used the Congress of Vienna's own principles against the Quadruple Alliance, arguing that Russia's aggrandizement at the expense of the Ottoman Empire violated the balance of power in the East. After precipitating a diplomatic crisis that lead to the outbreak of the Crimean War, France joined the war on behalf of the Ottoman Empire against Russia and convinced Great Britain to do the same. For the first time since the Napoleonic Wars, French troops fought a European opponent and won. By defeating Russia in the Crimean War, Napoleon III had simultaneously shored up his popularity at home, humbled a foe, and cemented his alliance with Great Britain.

With Russia sidelined and Britain befriended, Napoleon III looked next to hobble the Austrian Empire. A big, unwieldy, multi-ethnic construct, Austria represented everything that was wrong with Old Europe to a modern nationalist leader like Napoleon III. While Austria regained its lost Italian territories at the Congress of Vienna and ensured, in Austrian minister Metternich's words, that Italy remained only a "geographical expression," the various tiny states of the peninsula never forgot their brief unity under Napoleon.

As a young man, Louis-Napoleon spent much of his time in Italy and became involved in the Carbonari, a pro-Italian unification group fighting against Austrian oppression. The savvy Camillo Cavour, prime minister of the most powerful Italian state, the Kingdom of Sardinia-Piedmont, aggressively courted Napoleon III for his support in a war against Austria – even committing an expeditionary force of 18,000 troops to the Crimean War. In the summer of 1859, Napoleon III and Cavour signed a secret treaty whereby France would join Sardinia-Piedmont in a war against Austria in exchange for the provinces of Savoy and Nice. While ultimately successful, the high causalities suffered by the French at the Battle of Solferino (which led to the establishment of both the Geneva Conventions and the International Red Cross) and the subsequent Italian annexation of the Papal States led to widespread disapproval at home, particularly amongst conservatives.

Napoleon III's penchant for foreign policy adventurism extended far beyond the borders of Europe. Believing that France had to catch up to Britain in the race for colonies, he escalated a conflict over Catholic missionaries in Southeast Asia, precipitating a full-scale invasion of Vietnam in 1861. The French would remain in control of that country (later combined with Cambodia and Laos as French Indochina) until their defeat at the Battle of Dien Bien Phu by the Communist forces of Ho Chi Minh in 1954. Imperial France also tried to assert itself in Asia by joining with Britain against the Chinese Empire in the Second Opium War, launching punitive expeditions against the hermit kingdom of Korea, annexing Tahiti, and sending military advisors to Japan to train the forces of the Shogun in their war against the Emperor.

The outbreak of the American Civil War in 1861 presented Napoleon III with a unique opportunity. With the United States distracted, he could intervene in the Americas with impunity. For most of the 19th-century European powers abided by the Monroe Doctrine, which declared the Western Hemisphere closed to further colonization. Now, Napoleon III saw his chance to secure an expanded French role on the far side of the Atlantic. His 'Grand Scheme for the Americas' consisted of two parts: 1) support the Confederate States of America in an attempt to gain a new ally; and 2) install a friendly regime in Mexico. Neither objective met with much success.

The French textile industry depended heavily on cheap cotton imports from America, so the U.S.-imposed embargo on southern ports during the Civil War precipitated an industrial crisis, putting pressure on Napoleon III to force a quick resolution to the conflict. While he toyed with the idea of granting full diplomatic recognition to the Confederate States, he knew that doing so risked war with the United States and would not take the plunge unless Great Britain joined him. The Confederate defeat at the battle of Gettysburg in 1863 ended any serious chance of direct European intervention, but the French shipbuilding firm L'Arman did construct an ironclad warship for the South in 1864, the *CSS Stonewall.* While greatly feared by the Union navy, she never had a chance to fire a shot in anger. By the time the *Stonewall* made it across the Atlantic in 1865, the war was over.

The Mexican intervention was even more of a debacle. In 1861, President Benito Juárez announced his intention to suspend interest payments on Mexico's crushing debt, enraging her creditors in Britain, Spain, and France. The always-opportunistic Napoleon III used this as a *causus belli* to justify invading Mexico and installing a pro-French regime in North America. On June 7, 1863, Mexico City fell to French forces, and three days later they established a puppet state, the Empire of Mexico, with Austrian Archduke Ferdinand Maximilian offered the throne as Emperor Maximilian I. His tumultuous four-year reign was characterized

by civil war against republican forces at home and disdain abroad. The United States never recognized the Mexican Empire, and after the defeat of the Confederacy in 1865, demanded that France remove her troops from North America immediately. With his hopes for a friendly Confederate States and Mexican Empire dashed, Napoleon III conceded to American demands, leaving his brother Emperor to his fate. Captured by republican forces on May 15, 1867, the newly restored President Juárez wanted to send a message to France that he would not tolerate foreign intervention in Mexican affairs. On June 19, the unfortunate Emperor Maximilian I was put to death by firing squad.

For all his epic failures in foreign policy, Napoleon III's domestic reforms lasted far longer than he did – although like everything else in his reign they were accompanied by controversy. The Emperor's primary goal was to make France the economic equal of Great Britain and the United States. Bucking the tradition of economic protectionism, Napoleon III believed that foreign competition would make domestic industries more efficient and competitive in the long run. In 1860, he ratified the Cobden-Chevalier Treaty, the first ever free trade agreement between Britain and France. He also saw the State as an economic partner with private industry, encouraging the creation of investment banks like Société Générale and using public funds to fuel infrastructure spending on rail lines and port expansions for steamliners. Perhaps the most ambitious public works project of the Second Empire was the construction of the Suez Canal in Egypt, which opened for shipping in 1869.

The Emperor also had a distinctly progressive streak when it came to education. He massively increased the budget for public schools, seeing an educated workforce as essential for success in the 19th century. New research universities sprung up all across the country, and for the first time they admitted women as well. As a testament to Napoleon III's educational reforms, the literacy rate in France rose from under 50% in 1852 to nearly 75% by 1870.

The Second Empire's most enduring impact on the face of modern France was the renovation of Paris, carried out by Baron Haussmann. Paris in 1850 was still very much a medieval city filled with crowded tenements and narrow, winding streets. As part of his overall push to industrialize the country, Napoleon III wanted to turn Paris into a gleaming modern capital, eliminating the dark, congested, and generally unhygienic city center. An added benefit was that troops could move more easily through wide thoroughfares, enabling the government to put down riots with greater ease. The wide boulevards, spacious public squares, iconic facades, and plentiful green spaces Paris is known for today all stem from Haussmann's renovations.

The doom of Napoleon III's regime came from the one rival power he neither humbled nor befriended: Prussia. Since becoming Prime Minister of Prussia in 1862, Otto von Bismarck had masterfully played the game of European grand diplomacy, with his ultimate goal being the unification of the various German states into one united empire. Following the Crimean War's dismantling of the Concert of Europe, Bismarck moved to challenge Austria's traditional leadership role in Germany. Announcing that the

165

question of German unification would not be answered by speeches, but with "blood and iron," he drove Prussia into war with Austria in 1866 – a war they won handily. Austria's defeat left Prussia as the undisputed power in Germany, but Bismarck knew he needed a war against a major foreign rival to bring the various states together, and that rival was France.

In order to unite the German states in a common cause he needed to make France the aggressor. In 1870, Bismarck floated the idea of placing a member of the Prussian royal family on the vacant throne of Spain, knowing that such an idea would terrify Napoleon III. The Emperor sent the French ambassador, Count Benedetti, to voice his concerns to King Wilhelm I of Prussia. Bismarck tinkered with the wording of the diplomatic report, making it look as if the King rudely dismissed Benedetti and put Napoleon III's honor at issue for the world to see. The ploy worked. French forces mobilized immediately in a show of force, which caused Prussia to mobilize as well. Six days later, after Prussia refused to demobilize, France declared war. The other German states quickly allied with Prussia just like Bismarck had planned.

Most military experts at the time assumed a French victory, or at least a close contest. The results were exactly the opposite, and shook the European establishment to its core. Prussia's large and modern army overwhelmed the French and quickly occupied the northern part of the country. After suffering a string of defeats, Napoleon III took personal command of his army and led it straight into a trap at the Battle of Sedan. With his forces completely surrounded, the Prussians pounced. General Auguste-Alexandre Ducrot expertly summed up the dire situation of the French army with the observation, "We are in the chamber pot

and about to be shit upon." By the day's end, France would suffer one of the worst defeats in her history, losing the entire army with the Emperor himself taken as a prisoner of war. When word of Napoleon III's capture reached Paris on September 4, 1870, republicans and radicals stormed the Hôtel de Ville, announcing the end of the Second Empire and restoration of the Republic. With the incarcerated Emperor unable to enforce his own rule, the regime collapsed like a house of cards. It is a fitting testament to the chaos of the Revolutions that Louis-Napoleon of House Bonaparte had the distinction of serving as both France's first president and final monarch.

NAPOLEON III's
ITALIAN MISTRESS

Cavour had become Prime Minister of the Kingdom of Sardinia-Piedmont soon after it had suffered two crushing defeats to the Austrian Empire. His tiny kingdom needed a strong ally if it hoped to unite Italy, and the adventurous French Emperor seemed the most likely candidate. Cavour made all the right political moves by supporting France in the Crimean War and promising it lost territory in exchange for an alliance, but he knew that winning over Napoleon III would require a more personal touch. In 1855, Cavour travelled to Paris to seek an audience with the Emperor. Accompanying him on this trip was his cousin Virginia Oldoini, the Countess of Castiglione. Regarded as one of the most beautiful women in Europe at the time, she was sent to encourage the Emperor to see the benefits of siding with Sardinia-Piedmont, and given instructions to "succeed by whatever means you wish, but succeed." And succeed she did when she piqued Napoleon III's interest at an imperial ball by wearing her famously scandalous 'Queen of Hearts' costume. The two struck up a relationship and she took up residence in Paris as the Emperor's mistress for the next three years. During her time at court, Virginia became one of Europe's first photographic models, posing for hundreds of pictures (this was during a time when photographs were so expensive that even rich people might only sit for a couple of them over their entire lifetime). While their relationship ended in 1857, her influence with Napoleon III helped to secure the alliance between France and Sardinia-Piedmont, which lead to the unification of Italy as a single county. She repaid the favor to her imperial paramour several years later when she convinced Otto von Bismarck not to occupy Paris after the German victory at the Battle of Sedan.

XIX

FIGHTING GERMANS AND COMMUNISTS:
THE TWENTIETH CENTURY BECKONS

he newly created emergency 'Government of National Defense' organized an armed resistance against Prussia during the ensuing siege of Paris, but it was only a matter of time before France capitulated. On January 28, 1871, with all hope of relief exhausted, Paris surrendered. Bismarck's dream of a unified Germany finally became a reality, with the King of Prussia assuming the title Kaiser Wilhelm I of the German Empire in the Hall of Mirrors at Versailles. Germany forced France to sign a humiliating peace treaty to end the war (against Bismarck's advice), requiring her to pay a huge indemnity and give up her provinces of Alsace and Lorraine along the Rhine River. From that day forward, French schoolchildren were taught to avenge this defeat and reclaim the lost provinces, which they finally did in 1918, forcing a defeated Germany to sign the equally punitive Treaty of Versailles in the very same Hall of Mirrors.

Elections in February returned a conservative majority to the National Assembly with Adolphe Thiers as their leader. Paris, meanwhile, remained an armed camp under control of the National Guard militia who defended the city during the siege. Radical and socialist elements had taken over running the city and infiltrated the Guard, essentially turning it into their enforcement arm. The Guard remained hostile to the newly conservative national government, and refused to turn over their arms. When Thiers sent in regular army troops to seize the nearly 400 cannon under the Guard's control, heated passions turned to violence. A sizeable number,

Adolphe Thiers

possibly even the majority, of the troops defected to the side of the Guards and executed their commanding officers. Fearing further troop defections, Thiers ordered all government forces to abandon Paris, leaving the Guard in complete control of the capital. Socialist leaders and the National Guard took the opportunity to declare a full insurrection against the central government, organizing themselves as the Paris Commune once again.

For the first time since their defeat in the June Days Uprising more than twenty years earlier, Parisian radicals (calling themselves Communards) saw the opportunity to establish their dreamed-of Democratic and Social Republic. Out went the tricolor; in came the red flag. The Gregorian Calendar got the axe in exchange for the Republican Calendar, defunct since 1805. The Communal Council issued a whirlwind of decrees: they seized Church property, suspended delinquent rent and debt payments, granted pensions to National Guardsmen, regulated work hours, and guaranteed the right of workers to take over abandoned businesses. In later years Karl Marx would wax poetic about the efforts of the Communards to create the first worker's state in an industrialized country, and future Communist leaders Lenin and Mao formulated their strategies based on the experiences of the Paris Commune.

The Commune was hardly able to focus on governing as Paris was placed under siege once again, this time by government forces. Throughout the months of April and May, the surrounding suburbs turned into war zones as Thiers increased his stranglehold on the city. Socialist political clubs and trade union organizations from throughout the world expressed their support, but provided precious little in the way of actual relief. In late May, government forces opened a breach in the walls and occupied the more sympathetic western parts of the city. The Commune authorized the creation of a new Committee of Public Safety to deal with the crisis, but it was already too late. The intense urban combat to follow would be the deadliest Paris would see throughout the entire Revolutionary period, earning it the name *La Semaine Sanglante,* the Bloody Week.

Haussmann's renovations of Paris served their intended purpose, restricting the ability of Communards to form defensive barricades while allowing government troops to march around the city in formation. Atrocities abounded on both sides. The army shot suspected Communards on sight, with some summary executions numbering hundreds at a time. The Communards took hostages, mostly clergymen, civil servants, and those otherwise favorable to the government, and executed them in retribution. Unlike prior revolts, Government forces used heavy artillery to blast buildings fortified by the Commune, while the Communards set explosives in sewers and threw Molotov cocktails, burning down the Tuileries, Hôtel de Ville, Louvre, and Palais de Justice. By the time the fighting ended on May 28, Paris was a rubble-strewn, burnt-out shell of itself, and while there is no complete list, the estimated casualty numbers are all quite high, possibly topping 20,000 dead and wounded with several thousand more deported to penal colonies.

The bloody end of the Paris Commune represented the last spasm of the French Revolutions. After eighty years of turmoil, it was as if all those revolutionary animal spirits were finally exhausted. While never popular, and constantly threatened by both monarchists on the right and socialists on the left, the majority of the French people settled on establishing a Third Republic as the "form of government which divides us least," in the words of Thiers. It would last for the next seventy years, until its collapse in 1940, after defeat by Nazi Germany.

XX

THE END OF A WILD RIDE:

THE LEGACY OF

THE FRENCH REVOLUTIONS

We began our journey in the gilded ballrooms of Versailles under the reign of Louis XVI and here is where we end, with the modern world of La Belle Époque Paris right around the corner. Before we finish, let's take a moment to reflect on how far we've come.

It's not an exaggeration to say that most of the 19th and 20th centuries were shaped, directly or indirectly, by the French Revolutions. Major social and political movements as far ranging as the abolition of slavery, formation of labor unions, extension of the franchise, women's suffrage, public education, de-colonization, and the worldwide spread of liberal democracy were all the progeny of the French Revolutions. Not everything it unleashed was joy and light of course. There was also a dark side, characterized by an authoritarian streak and organized political violence on previously unimaginable scales. Both the ideologies of Communism and Fascism, with their desire for a break with the past and creation of an idealized New Society and New Man, owe much to the Revolutions.

The French Revolutions have left such a lasting impact on our cultural consciousness that we still read *A Tale of Two Cities* and *War and Peace*, pay money to watch Russell Crowe sing in *Les Misérables* or eat a dessert named after the Emperor Napoleon. More than 200 years after the fall of the Bastille, political commentator Ann Coulter can still stir the passions of her readers by describing the French Revolution as "the godless antithesis to the founding of America." To realize just how remarkable it is that everyone understands the reference (if not the sentiment), think about how few historical events from 18th-century Europe this would work with. It's a good bet you'll never read an op-ed piece equating America's military struggles abroad with a failure to properly learn the lessons of the War of Spanish Succession.

Yes, the legacy of the Revolutions remains with us today, along with all their ironies and paradoxes. We see it both when an oppressed people rise up against an authoritarian regime demanding recognition of their rights, and when a military strongman overthrows an elected government, claiming to represent the will of the people against corrupt and self-serving politicians. The very concepts of 'conservatism' and 'liberalism' largely derive from whether one was supportive of or opposed to the ideals of the Revolutions, and have become so ingrained that nearly all modern societies still use them as a common point of reference – a kind of political Planck's constant. Think of all the questions raised by the Revolutions that we're still struggling with today: What is the proper relationship between the State and the individual? How should wealth be distributed across society? To what extent should tradition be either respected or discarded? What should the public role of religion be, if any? Should power be centralized or decentralized? To what degree is authoritarianism acceptable if it preserves social order?

While it might sound strange, the events are still too close in time and the conflicts too raw for us to evaluate dispassionately. What is the lasting impact of the French Revolutions? When a reporter once asked Chinese Premier Zhou Enlai this question, his famous response perhaps summed it up best: "Too soon to say."

SACRÉ-COEUR AND THE
END OF REVOLUTIONS

While less emblematic than the Eiffel Tower, La Basilique du Sacré-Coeur occupies a prominent place in the Paris skyline, situated on the city's highest point on the hill of Montmartre. What most people don't realize when they gaze upon the soaring domes of the basilica is that they are looking not only at a church, but at a monument – a pure, white beacon symbolizing the triumph of the conservative order. Unlike the centuries-old Notre-Dame cathedral, Sacré-Coeur is a relative newcomer, construction only having finished in 1914 (although it wasn't formally consecrated until 1919, after the First World War was over). Following France's humiliating defeat in the Franco-Prussian War and the ensuing violence of the Paris Commune, the Catholic Church and its conservative allies were once again resurgent. Seeing these terrible events as divine chastisement for France's sins, the bishops pressed for the construction of a grand church on the Montmartre hill as a form of national penance, marking a definitive break with the era of revolutions and a return to a "Government of Moral Order." The Third Republic acquired the territory and gave it to the church for construction of the basilica, which commenced in 1875. So that there was no mistake about the nationalist/royalist/religious symbolism of Sacré-Coeur, two equestrian statues of saints were installed by the front entrance: one of St. Louis (King Louis IX), and the other of St. Joan of Arc (this wasn't the only example of the Third Republic attempting to suppress the memories of the last century by appealing to patriotic and religious sentiments through public artwork – Emmanuel Frémiet's romantic bronze statue of Joan of Arc in the Place des Pyramides sounds out as well). As a testament to the strong passions the building still invokes, in 1971, during the centennial of the Paris Commune, a group of radicals occupied the basilica and called for revolution before being chased out by the police. Five years later a bomb exploded inside the church, causing extensive damage to one of the domes. Allegedly, a single red rose was left on the grave of Louis Blanqui in Père Lachaise Cemetery immediately following the incident.

WORKS CONSULTED

Andress, David. *The Terror: The Merciless War for Freedom in Revolutionary France.* New York: Farrar, Straus, and Giroux, 2007.

Bell, David A. *The First Total War: Napoleon's Europe and the Birth of Modern Warfare as We Know it.* New York: Houghton Mifflin Company, 2007.

Bergeron, Louis. *France Under Napoleon.* Princeton: Princeton University Press, 1981.

Blanning, T. C. W. *The Nineteenth Century: Europe 1789-1914.* Oxford New York: Oxford University Press, 2000.

Burke, Edmund, and L. G. Mitchell. *Reflections on the Revolution in France.* Oxford: Oxford University Press, 2009.

Bresler, Fenton S. *Napoleon III: A Life.* New York: Carroll & Graf, 1999.

Carlyle, Thomas. *The French Revolution: A History.* New York: Modern Library, 2002.

Donegan, C. F. "Dr. Guillotin – Reformer and Humanitarian." *Journal of the Royal Society of Medicine* 83 : 637-639.

Doyle, William. *The Oxford History of the French Revolution.* Oxford: Oxford University Press, 2002.

Dwyer, Philip G. *Citizen Emperor: Napoleon in Power.* New Haven: Yale University Press, 2013.

Englund, Steven. *Napoleon: A Political Life.* Cambridge: Harvard University Press, 2004.

Figes, Orlando. *The Crimean War: A History.* New York: Picador, 2012.

Gildea, Robert. *Children of the Revolution: The French, 1799-1914.* Cambridge: Harvard University Press, 2008.

Harvey, David. "Monument and Myth." *Annals of the Association of American Geographers* 69, no. 3 (September 1979): 362-381.

Herold, J C. *The Age of Napoleon.* New York: Mariner Books, 2002.

Hibbert, Christopher. *The Days of the French Revolution.* New York: Morrow Quill Paperbacks, 1981.

Horne, Alistair. *The Fall of Paris: The Siege and the Commune 1870-71.* London: Penguin, 2007.

Israel, Jonathan. *Revolutionary Ideas: An Intellectual History of the French Revolution from the Rights of Man to Robespierre.* Princeton: Princeton University Press, 2014.

Israel, Jonathan. *A Revolution of the Mind: Radical Enlightenment and the Intellectual Origins of Modern Democracy.* Princeton: Princeton University Press, 2010.

Kirkland, Stephane. *Paris Reborn: Napoléon III, Baron Haussmann, and the Quest to Build a Modern City.* New York: St. Martin's Press, 2013.

Kissinger, Henry. *A World Restored; Metternich, Castlereagh, and the Problems of Peace, 1812-22.* Boston: Houghton Mifflin, 1973.

Lyons, Martyn. *Napoleon Bonaparte and the Legacy of the French Revolution.* New York: St. Martin's Press, 1994.

Mason, Laura, and Tracey Rizzo. *The French Revolution: A Document Collection.* Boston: Houghton Mifflin, 1999.

Napoleon, and Somerset S. Chair. *Napoleon on Napoleon: An Autobiography of the Emperor.* New York: Sterling Pub. Co, 1992.

Palmer, R. R. *Twelve Who Ruled: The Year of the Terror in the French Revolution.* Princeton: Princeton University Press, 2005.

Schama, Simon. *Citizens: A Chronicle of the French Revolution.* London: Penguin, 2004.

Scurr, Ruth. Fatal Purity: *Robespierre and the French Revolution.* New York: H. Holt, 2007.

Strayer, Joseph. *On the Medieval Origins of the Modern State*. Princeton: Princeton University Press, 1970.

Tocqueville, Gerald E. Bevan, and Hugh Brogan. *The Ancien Régime and the French Revolution*. London: Penguin, 2008.

Tuchman, Barbara W. *A Distant Mirror: The Calamitous 14th Century*. New York: Ballantine, 1979.

Wetzel, David. *A Duel of Giants: Bismarck, Napoleon III, and the Origins of the Franco-Prussian War*. Madison: University of Wisconsin Press, 2001.

ABOUT THE AUTHOR

MIKE LaMONICA is a graduate of the University of Mary Washington where he earned a B.A. in History and was inducted into the National History Honor Society. He subsequently attended Quinnipiac University School of Law where he obtained his J.D. and acted as an editor for the Quinnipiac Probate Law Journal. He currently practices law full-time at the Connecticut Attorney General's Office and is a part-time professor of English at Quinnipiac University.

ABOUT THE ARTIST

MOTLEY's previous illustrated books include *The Golden Ass of Lucius Apuleius* (David R Godine) and *The One Marvelous Thing* (Dalkey Archive Press). His *Tragic Strip* appears monthly in *The Brooklyn Rail.* He's a core contributor to the indie anthology *Cartozia Tales.* He teaches cartooning at the School of Visual Arts and illustration at Pratt Manhattan. Visit T. Motley's website at www.tmotley.com.

THE FOR BEGINNERS® SERIES

AFRICAN HISTORY FOR BEGINNERS	ISBN 978-1-934389-18-8
ANARCHISM FOR BEGINNERS	ISBN 978-1-934389-32-4
ARABS & ISRAEL FOR BEGINNERS	ISBN 978-1-934389-16-4
ART THEORY FOR BEGINNERS	ISBN 978-1-934389-47-8
ASTRONOMY FOR BEGINNERS	ISBN 978-1-934389-25-6
AYN RAND FOR BEGINNERS	ISBN 978-1-934389-37-9
BARACK OBAMA FOR BEGINNERS, AN ESSENTIAL GUIDE	ISBN 978-1-934389-44-7
BEN FRANKLIN FOR BEGINNERS	ISBN 978-1-934389-48-5
BLACK HISTORY FOR BEGINNERS	ISBN 978-1-934389-19-5
THE BLACK HOLOCAUST FOR BEGINNERS	ISBN 978-1-934389-03-4
BLACK WOMEN FOR BEGINNERS	ISBN 978-1-934389-20-1
CHOMSKY FOR BEGINNERS	ISBN 978-1-934389-17-1
DADA & SURREALISM FOR BEGINNERS	ISBN 978-1-934389-00-3
DANTE FOR BEGINNERS	ISBN 978-1-934389-67-6
DECONSTRUCTION FOR BEGINNERS	ISBN 978-1-934389-26-3
DEMOCRACY FOR BEGINNERS	ISBN 978-1-934389-36-2
DERRIDA FOR BEGINNERS	ISBN 978-1-934389-11-9
EASTERN PHILOSOPHY FOR BEGINNERS	ISBN 978-1-934389-07-2
EXISTENTIALISM FOR BEGINNERS	ISBN 978-1-934389-21-8
FANON FOR BEGINNERS	ISBN 978-1-934389-87-4
FDR AND THE NEW DEAL FOR BEGINNERS	ISBN 978-1-934389-50-8
FOUCAULT FOR BEGINNERS	ISBN 978-1-934389-12-6
GENDER & SEXUALITY FOR BEGINNERS	ISBN 978-1-934389-69-0
GLOBAL WARMING FOR BEGINNERS	ISBN 978-1-934389-27-0
GREEK MYTHOLOGY FOR BEGINNERS	ISBN 978-1-934389-83-6
HEIDEGGER FOR BEGINNERS	ISBN 978-1-934389-13-3
THE HISTORY OF CLASSICAL MUSIC FOR BEGINNERS	ISBN 978-1-939994-26-4
THE HISTORY OF OPERA FOR BEGINNERS	ISBN 978-1-934389-79-9
ISLAM FOR BEGINNERS	ISBN 978-1-934389-01-0
JANE AUSTEN FOR BEGINNERS	ISBN 978-1-934389-61-4
JUNG FOR BEGINNERS	ISBN 978-1-934389-76-8
KIERKEGAARD FOR BEGINNERS	ISBN 978-1-934389-14-0
LACAN FOR BEGINNERS	ISBN 978-1-934389-39-3
LINGUISTICS FOR BEGINNERS	ISBN 978-1-934389-28-7
MALCOLM X FOR BEGINNERS	ISBN 978-1-934389-04-1
MARX'S DAS KAPITAL FOR BEGINNERS	ISBN 978-1-934389-59-1
MCLUHAN FOR BEGINNERS	ISBN 978-1-934389-75-1
NIETZSCHE FOR BEGINNERS	ISBN 978-1-934389-05-8
PAUL ROBESON FOR BEGINNERS	ISBN 978-1-934389-81-2
PHILOSOPHY FOR BEGINNERS	ISBN 978-1-934389-02-7
PLATO FOR BEGINNERS	ISBN 978-1-934389-08-9
POETRY FOR BEGINNERS	ISBN 978-1-934389-46-1
POSTMODERNISM FOR BEGINNERS	ISBN 978-1-934389-09-6
RELATIVITY & QUANTUM PHYSICS FOR BEGINNERS	ISBN 978-1-934389-42-3
SARTRE FOR BEGINNERS	ISBN 978-1-934389-15-7
SHAKESPEARE FOR BEGINNERS	ISBN 978-1-934389-29-4
STRUCTURALISM & POSTSTRUCTURALISM FOR BEGINNERS	ISBN 978-1-934389-10-2
WOMEN'S HISTORY FOR BEGINNERS	ISBN 978-1-934389-60-7
UNIONS FOR BEGINNERS	ISBN 978-1-934389-77-5
U.S. CONSTITUTION FOR BEGINNERS	ISBN 978-1-934389-62-1
ZEN FOR BEGINNERS	ISBN 978-1-934389-06-5
ZINN FOR BEGINNERS	ISBN 978-1-934389-40-9

WWW.FORBEGINNERSBOOKS.COM